THE AUTHOR'S GUIDE TO EBOOK BUNDLING

CHUCK HEINTZELMAN

KP

For Tina

Thanks for putting up with me during my obsession with bundling

CONTENTS

The Magic of a Bundle   vii

Why This Book?   1

PART ONE
BUNDLING IN THE WILD

1. What is an Ebook Bundle?   7
2. Why Bundle?   13
3. Example Bundles   17
4. Building a Single Author Bundle With Vellum   23
5. The Problems with Multi-Author Bundles   37
6. Building Multi-Author Bundles   41
7. Delivering Bundles to Customers   51
8. Types of Readers   57
9. Pricing and Selling Bundles   63
10. Box Set Images   71
11. Bundling as a Mini-Community   83
12. Bundling for Discoverability   89

PART TWO
BUNDLING AT BUNDLERABBIT

13. Components of BundleRabbit   99
14. What Authors Need   105
15. What Curators Do   113
16. Services BundleRabbit Provides   119
17. Tips for Getting Into a Bundle   125
18. The BundleRabbit Mini-Community   131
19. Additional Discoverability   137

Where To Go Next   145

Also by Chuck Heintzelman   149
About the Author   151
About BundleRabbit   153
Example Bundles at BundleRabbit   155

THE MAGIC OF A BUNDLE

BY DEAN WESLEY SMITH

A number of years back I had the pleasure of talking with Chuck Heintzelman about the idea of starting his wonderful BundleRabbit business. As I told Chuck then (and still believe), he is one of the few people on the planet with all the combined skills it takes to put together such a business

You see, Chuck is an amazing computer person in his day job. But when he puts on his creative hat and hits the fiction-writing computer, his short stories are stunning.

So for me, to have him even want my opinion on something he was doing was an honor.

But as we talked, Chuck kept confusing me. I was familiar with the other forms of bundling, meaning single author bundles and multi-author bundles through other bundling sites. And it seemed on the surface that was where Chuck was headed with his new idea. Yet I was confused.

Now understand, I might be in my mid-sixties, but I am not often confused when it comes to publishing things. Life things, sure, but publishing, not so much, since I have worked and made my living in this business for forty years now.

Yet with Chuck's idea, I just kept getting more and more unsure what he was even talking about. Finally, after numbers of e-mails and a few in-person conversations, I finally got through my thick skull that what Chuck was trying to do wasn't something anyone had done before in publishing.

Or that any other bundling business actually had even come close to trying.

Chuck was aiming at something brand new. And so far beyond my imagination of computer skills as to seem magical.

No wonder I was confused.

To put it simply, Chuck wanted to develop a platform to sell multi-author bundles. I got that. A number of other platforms do that already.

But Chuck wanted the authors to do it themselves, unlike other platforms where the bundles are strictly controlled and put together behind the scenes.

Chuck developed the programming and the business structure to let authors invite other authors to be part of a bundle of novels and simply be hosted on BundleRabbit.

And he set up a library of submitted work, where someone

THE MAGIC OF A BUNDLE

wanting to put together a bundle could go pick stories even if that moderator didn't know the author of the work.

And he allowed short stories to be part of the library as well as novels.

He also developed the software so that there was no limit on the number of bundles that could be running at any one point. So the larger the group of moderators and the group of authors with work in the library, the more bundles there would be.

That would then be better for the readers.

Because that's really where the genius of Chuck's idea sits. In the old ways of publishing, there were always gatekeepers to keep books and stories away from readers. Someone's judgment got in the way of what a reader might like.

In more traditional multi-author bundling, those gatekeepers are the moderators and the owner of the business.

In BundleRabbit there is none of that. Only someone's imagination and drive to put together groups of stories limit what readers can find through BundleRabbit.

My old mind couldn't grasp that Chuck was trying (and has now managed) to set up total freedom for bundles. That somehow he has done the massive programming that allows such bundling to even happen seamlessly.

During the entire building process over the last few years, Chuck has learned the ins and outs of bundles, both single-author bundles and multi-author bundles.

What you will get in this book will help you understand all

different levels of bundles and how to not only put them together with your own work for yourself, but how to get with other authors to combine promotion and discoverability power to help readers find your work.

So it is my honor to introduce this book and give you a glimpse into the fantastic and inventive mind of Chuck Heintzelman.

Enjoy.

Dean Wesley Smith

WHY THIS BOOK?

FIRST OF ALL, THERE'S NOTHING AVAILABLE LIKE THIS book. I could not find a single, decent book on ebook bundling that defined what bundling is, how to do it, and the pitfalls to watch out for. Ebook bundling is becoming more and more prevalent in today's market, yet nobody has thoroughly tackled the topic and shared what they've discovered.

Second, this topic is of particular importance to me because I created BundleRabbit.com, an ebook bundling platform. It should be a relevant topic for every indie author because the number of ebook bundles available in the marketplace grows daily. Ebook bundling is another sales tool that more and more authors are making use of.

- Ebook bundling is a great way for authors to increase their discoverability.

- Bundling allows authors to uniquely combine existing products (novels, short stories, etc.) into new packages, creating even more products.
- Best of all, bundling creates additional income streams for authors.

MY BACKGROUND

Okay, here's the obligatory blah, blah, blah about me. Where I tell you a bit about my background and how ebook bundling became important to me.

Many authors recognize their calling at an early age. They seem to be born with a quill in their hand. Not me. I didn't spring from the head of Zeus as a fully formed author (as a friend of mine likes to say.) Nope. I started as a computer nerd. I suppose I still am one.

Back in 1980, when I was in the 9th grade (you do the math if you want to figure out my age), I took my first computer class. Immediately, I was hooked. It was so cool to be able to make this machine do what I wanted it to do. I'd often *time warp* while writing code, the hours slipping away while I was creating a program.

Fast-forward 25 years. After creating dozens of computer systems, in many different computer languages, I found designing and writing software was getting a bit boring. I'd become quite successful in my field and the challenge wasn't there any longer. So I tried writing fiction.

Bam!

Just like those early days of coding, I was hooked. I started time warping while writing fiction, something I'd never experienced except through coding.

At this point I started seeing myself as both a *Software Developer* and a *Short Story Hobbyist* and not so much as a computer nerd (although my family would probably disagree with that).

Then, in 2015, I noticed there were only two companies selling ebook bundles with regular success: StoryBundle and Humble Bundle.

I really liked what these companies were doing, but thought it would be even better if, instead of relying on a third-party to bundle one of my books, I could do it myself. I wanted a DIY ebook bundler. My vision was to create a marketplace where any indie author could submit their novels or short stories, allowing curators to come in and bundle stories to sell from this marketplace.

Thus BundleRabbit was born, the world's first DIY Ebook Bundling Platform. BundleRabbit launched on April 15th, 2016, and has been growing steadily and improving ever since.

So now I see myself as *Chuck from BundleRabbit* and a professional short story writer. But, yeah, I'm still a software developer at heart.

HOW THIS BOOK IS ORGANIZED

This book is divided into two sections.

1. **Bundling in the Wild**. This section discusses

3

bundling in general, what it is, how to do it, things to watch out for.

2. **BundleRabbit Bundling**. This section explains how bundling works using the BundleRabbit platform.

What is not in this book is an exhaustive list of marketing techniques. A few promotion methods are mentioned at a surface level, but this is not a marketing book.

This book is a guide to ebook bundling.

PART ONE

BUNDLING IN THE WILD

What is an Ebook Bundle?

THE MOST BASIC BUND_E QUESTION

The answer is simply "a group of ebooks." Bundle is a pretty general term. Let's break bundles down by a few other names they're known by. I'm also including a few other relevant definitions below.

COLLECTIONS

Collections are bundles of work by a single author. The most common form is a short story collection. But you can also have novel or novella collections.

Collections are packaged together as a single ebook with a single volume. Usually there's a single copyright page listing all the works within the ebook and an introduction to the collection.

Often there's an introduction to, or other notes about, each story within the collection.

ANTHOLOGIES

Anthologies are the multi-author equivalent of a collection. The introduction is often written by the editor of the anthology.

VOLUME

The term *volume* is borrowed from print books. With print books, a volume identifies a single book that's part of a larger collection. For example, *Encyclopedia Britannica Vol. 5: Hermoup-Lally*.

When it comes to ebooks, a volume is a *distinct* book within the ebook. Often each volume within a multi-volume ebook (aka Box Set) is complete within itself with its own copyright page, title page, and author biography.

BOX SET

Box set (*or boxed set, the grammatically correct but less used term*) refers to how the bundle is packaged and presented. A box set is an ebook containing more than one volume.

Often the image associated with an electronic box set depicts a 3D version of what the box set would look like if it were a physical box set. See *Chapter 10 – Box Set Images* for examples.

BUNDLE

One of the definitions of a bundle focuses to how the ebooks within the bundle are delivered. Ebook bundling services such as BundleRabbit or StoryBundle provide bundles where each individual ebook can be downloaded separately. This is what many people think of when they think of an ebook bundle.

Here's where terminology can get murky. In my view, any group of ebooks sold together as a unit is a bundle. Period. Doesn't matter how they're delivered.

CROSS-POLLINATION

Cross-pollination loosely means sharing ideas, techniques, or knowledge between two or more sources for the betterment of each of the sources.

But in this book I'm specifically referring to cross-pollinating fans using multi-author bundles. In other words, you have the chance to be discovered by fans of other authors in your bundle, as they do by your fans.

OMNIBUS

A large bundle often containing all the volumes of a particular series. Usually by a single author, but occasionally a multi-author omnibus edition is created, especially in shared world series.

In rare cases, omnibus editions are not tied to a series, but contain all the works of a particular author; i.e. *The Omnibus Jules Verne.*

For very large, epic stories, you could even have multiple omnibuses. Think of a three-volume omnibus spanning of all the *Song of Ice and Fire* books (if George R.R. Martin ever finishes the series.)

❄

THE UNCOLLECTED ANTHOLOGY

Here's a unique take on bundles and anthologies...

Every three months, a group of writers write short stories centered around a common theme. They package their short stories individually but with common branding, and sell each book within the "anthology" separately.

Check it out at uncollectedanthology.com.

To me, this is a loosely coupled bundle.

❄

BUNDLES ALL THE WAY DOWN

Like I said, my view is that all these forms are bundles. Doesn't matter if there are multiple authors or a single author. Whether the bundle is comprised of a single ebook with a single volume, a multi-volume box set, or individual ebooks grouped together.

They're all bundles.

CHAPTER TWO
WHY BUNDLE?

> ❝ A man wrapped up in himself makes a very small bundle.

BENJAMIN FRANKLIN

THIS CHAPTER EXPLAINS WHY EBOOK BUNDLING IS IMPORTANT and why authors should do it.

MORE SALES

Whether it's having existing readers read more of your books or new readers discovering your books, it all comes down to one thing: more sales.

More sales equals more income.

Every other reason listed in this chapter is subordinate to this one, overarching goal of increasing sales. *This theme is repeated many times throughout this book.*

FROM THE AUTHOR'S PERSPECTIVE

As an author bundling your ebooks together, or bundling your books with others, what are the benefits?

- **More Inventory** – By bundling your ebooks together, you create additional inventory. You then have more products to sell.
- **Higher Priced Ebooks** – This benefit is often overlooked. Bundles sell at prices higher than individual ebooks, even with the discount. This gives you another price level in your sellable inventory.
- **Additional Income Streams** – Bundles allow you to repackage your existing ebooks (products) into new products. Yeah, yeah, that's already listed as *More Inventory*, but remember, a bundle is a new type of product, reaching new customers. It's a new income stream.
- **Cross Pollination** – With multi-author bundles, you're increasing your fan base by exposing your book to the fans of other authors.
- **Better Advertising ROI** – When you use paid advertising for your bundles, you get a better bang for your buck. Income from each bundle sale is higher than individual ebook sales.
- **More Marketing Strategies** – How about a *First in Series* bundle, including the first book of each of your series? What about a *Sampler Bundle* showcasing your work? Anything's possible.
- **Wider Audience** – Multi-author bundles, even

traditional ones such as anthologies, expand your audience.

FROM THE READER'S PERSPECTIVE

How about putting yourself in the reader's shoes. Why are bundles a benefit to readers?

- **Bundles are Great Deals** – They save customers money. Even higher priced bundles at 20% off of retail give customers a decent savings. Often readers can get bundles with deep discounts. Prices at 60%, 70%, even 80% off are not uncommon.
- **Bundles Allow Binge Reading** – We live in the age of Netflix. Consumers are binging on all types of entertainment. Even reading books.
- **Bundles Allow Discovery of New Writers** – A bundle reader will often come across a new reader they never would've normally found. This is always an exciting surprise to the dedicated reader.
- **Charities** – Many of the bundling services (such as Humble Bundle, BundleRabbit, and StoryBundle) allow a portion of each sale to be donated to charities. This gives the reader a good feeling. They're being socially responsible.
- **Helping Indie Authors** – Often with multi-author bundles, readers will recognize they're helping indie authors—another feel-good benefit.
- **Nonfiction Bundles for Research** – Each day more and more nonfiction bundles are available,

including titles such as *The Ultimate Digital Photography Bundle.* This allows readers to get a broad array of books on a single topic.

When readers are happy, they come back for more.

So you can see, both readers and authors benefit from bundles.

CHAPTER THREE
EXAMPLE BUNDLES

> Whether you're focused on increasing sales, expanding your line of products, or a particular promotion, it really comes down to one ultimate goal: having more readers read more of your fiction.
>
> THE PRIMARY REASON TO BUNDLE

IN THIS CHAPTER WE'LL LOOK AT A MYRIAD OF DIFFERENT types of bundles and how each is aimed at the goal of getting more readers. Keep in mind this list is by no means exhaustive. Creative people come up with new and different types of bundles all the time (as the authors in the Uncollected Anthology did).

SHORT STORY COLLECTION

If you have a number of short stories, it makes sense to bundle up these stories into collections. The effort to create a short story collection is low, and there are two major advantages to doing this:

1. Short story collections sell better than single short stories.
2. Increased inventory. Let's say you have 20 short stories. That's 20 different products. If you create four 5-story collections and two 10-story collections, you've increase your product count from 20 to 26. So without writing another story, you've increased your sellable products 30%.

NOVELLA COLLECTIONS OR BOX SETS

Just like a short story collections, but with slightly longer works. *Different Seasons* by Stephen King is a collection of four novellas.

TRILOGY AND SERIES BOX SETS

Like short story collections, but with novels. Some people call these novel collections, but the term *box set* is more descriptive since it denotes the multi-volume aspect of the ebook. (And really, you should make these ebooks multi-volume. It's very easy to do, as you'll learn later in this book.)

The term *box set* came from print book series that were literally a set of books inside a slipcase/box.

If you have a trilogy or quartet of novels available, but don't have the series available as a ebook box set, I urge you to add the following to your to-do list....

Create a multi-volume box set ASAP

You can get creative with series box sets. Say you have a 10-book series. You could break this into a 4-volume box set with two 3-volume box sets, or two 5-volume box sets. Regardless of how you divide the series, be sure to have the 10-volume omnibus edition.

When I read and like the first book in a series and go looking for book two in the series, I search for a box set of the series. If it's available, I'll often buy the box set.

Let's say each book in a trilogy is priced at $5.99 and the box set trilogy is priced at $11.99. That's only one penny more for me to pick up the box set rather than buying the next two novels individually. (*We'll get to pricing strategies later in this book.*) Sure, I'll effectively have two copies of the first novel, but if I reread the series, I'll go to the box set version.

❄

INTERESTING NOTE ABOUT NOVEL BOX SETS

I've talked to a number of authors about what happens to their sales figures after they introduce novel box sets. My expectation was that there'd be a decline in the individual novel sales. Surprisingly, every author I've spoken to said this is not the case, and that the box sets do not seem to diminish the individual sales.

This means the box sets are finding new readers, or at least introducing enough new readers to their single novel sales to offset those (like me) who move from purchasing the single novels to purchasing the box sets.

❄

SAMPLER COLLECTIONS

Another increasingly popular form of ebook collection is the *Sampler Collection*. If you write in several series, or across several genres, you can create a collection showcasing a sample of your work.

Fill this type of bundle with different short stories, or the first few chapters of several novels, or both. It's up to you. The goal here is to give readers a sampling of your work.

Sampler collections are a great email list builder. You can give your sampler collection to list subscribers as a free gift when they sign up.

FIRST IN SERIES BOX SET

Authors writing multiple series can create a *First in Series Box Set*. Bundle the first novel of each of your series together into one box set to offer readers a starting point into each of your series. The goal here is to get the reader interested enough to continue reading one or more of your series (perhaps in an omnibus edition).

First in Series collections aren't limited to a single author. If you're writing in a single series, you can still group together with other authors to offer a multi-author First in Series bundle. The advantage here is the cross-pollination of your fan bases.

ANTHOLOGIES

An anthology is a multi-author collection of short stories or short novels selected by the editor or compiler of the anthology.

Ebook Anthologies seem to becoming more popular the last few years. Just a personal observation. I have no sales figures to back this up, but there have been hundreds of anthologies on Kickstarter in the last two years alone.

Stories within anthologies usually are focused around a theme. Often there's one or two "big name" authors in an anthology. They serve the same purpose as anchor stores do in malls.

❋

A BUNDLE WITHIN A BUNDLE

Kevin J. Anderson recently curated *The Pulse Pounders Thriller Bundle*. This was a limited time bundle with many wonderful novels by authors including Kevin J. Anderson, Dean Wesley Smith, M.L. Buchman, J.F. Penn, and Jonathon Mayberry.

The bundle also contained the Fiction River *Pulse Pounders* anthology (which contained my story "Three Strikes"). So there you have it, a bundle (the anthology) within a bundle.

Consider bundling your own short story collection together with short story collections by other authors and you'll be in a bundle within a bundle.

❄

OMNIBUS BOX SETS

I've mentioned Omnibus editions several times so far in this book. This is where you bundle an entire series into one large, multi-volume ebook.

One of the best things about Omnibuses is they give you a very high-price item in your ebook inventory to sell. You may not be hitting the market at this price level.

And making upwards of $20 per sale can add up quickly. Some publishers are selling these massive box sets for well over $60 each.

CHAPTER FOUR
BUILDING A SINGLE AUTHOR
BUNDLE WITH VELLUM

66 Easily Create Beautiful Ebooks

VELLUM'S MOTTO

THIS CHAPTER PROVIDES A STEP-BY-STEP TUTORIAL ON USING *Vellum to create a short story collection. The same basic steps can be used to create larger box sets.*

ABOUT VELLUM

Vellum is Mac-only software that performs a single job, formatting ebooks. It does this job brilliantly.

Vellum's website is vellum.pub

Vellum compiles different versions of your ebook, each optimized for various retailers. (*iBooks, Kobo, Kindle, Nook, and*

Google Play at the time of this writing. There's also a Generic Epub version to use anywhere else.)

It creates these versions quickly with a single click of the mouse. And it optimizes the look and feel of your ebooks for the device they're read on. Thus if a reader views your ebook on an iPhone, it's just a clean as if they view the same ebook on a Kindle Paperwhite.

It's all about creating the best possible experience for the reader here.

It's not all rainbows and unicorns, though. There are a few negative things about Vellum. I'll list them at the end of this chapter.

❋

ATTENTION WINDOWS USERS

I know many authors who use Windows computers. Their entire writing, editing, and production process was in Windows. But when they saw Vellum and understood what it could do, they rushed out and bought a cheap, used Mac (about $200–$300) and now use Vellum to create their ebooks.

It really is that good.

❋

THE STEPS DETAILED BELOW GO THROUGH THE PROCESS OF creating a short story collection consisting of five short stories.

STEP 0 – PREP WORK

Before starting, I've created the following:

- A cover image for the collection.
- Five .DOCX files, one for each short story in the collection. Basically, the manuscript of each story with the title page removed.

Vellum's pretty good about detecting chapters. If there's a page break before the chapter, or the chapter title is centered and in bold text, Vellum will detect it and split the document into chapters correctly.

There's much more to importing...ornamental scene breaks, quoted text, and even using Vellum-specific styles in Word. You can find out these details on Vellum's website at help.vellum.pub/importing

I'll also be adding an ABOUT THE AUTHOR, COPYRIGHT, and ALSO BY pages to this collection, but for those I'll just copy and paste.

Also, because several of these short stories have small chapters instead of scenes, I've decided to have each short story as a separate volume within the collection.

STEP 1 – THE BOOK INFO

The first step after starting up Vellum and creating a new file is to enter the Book Info.

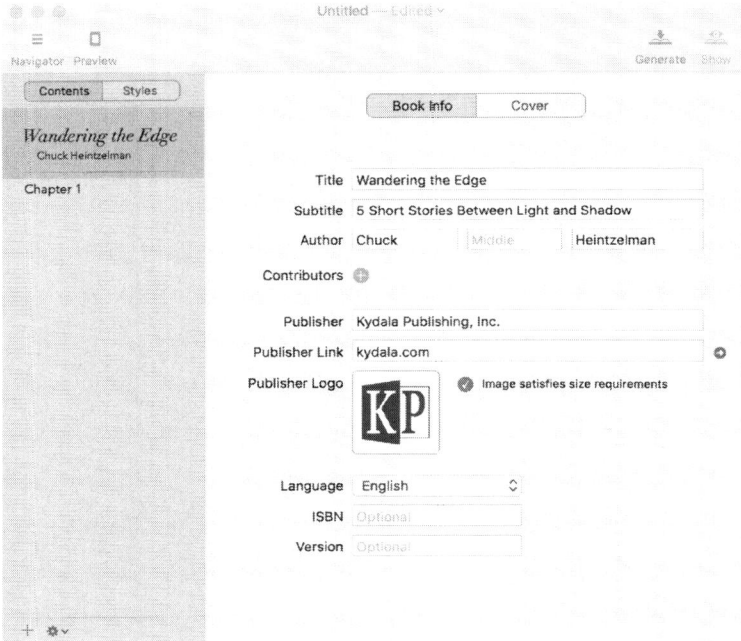

As you can see, in addition to Title, Subtitle, and Author, I also added my publisher information and logo.

Don't worry about the ISBN; there's no need for one with ebooks. But I did enter the Version as 1.0. (*If, after publication, I need to update this collection, iBooks requires the next version to be different.*)

STEP 2 – THE COVER

Next, I switched to the Cover tab to add the cover.

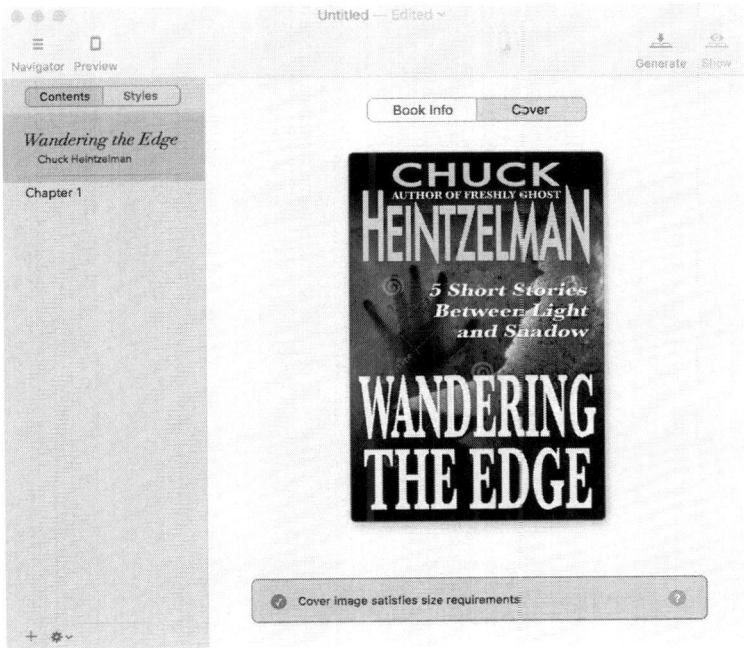

Vellum will tell you the cover image satisfies the size requirements. If you're using a 2:3 ratio cover, the minimum size is 1667 x 2500 pixels.

Before continuing I saved the Vellum file.

STEP 3 – CREATE THE EBOOK SKELETON

Next I created the skeleton of the ebook by adding all the top-level elements. I'm going to have the following elements in this collection:

1. Introduction (I'll write this later)
2. Short Story #1
3. Short Story #2
4. Short Story #3
5. Short Story #4
6. Short Story #5
7. An "About the Author" page
8. An "Also By" page
9. The Copyright page

When you create a new Vellum document, it starts off with an empty CHAPTER 1. I highlighted CHAPTER 1 and clicked the + at the bottom left corner of the window eight times to create a total of nine blank chapters.

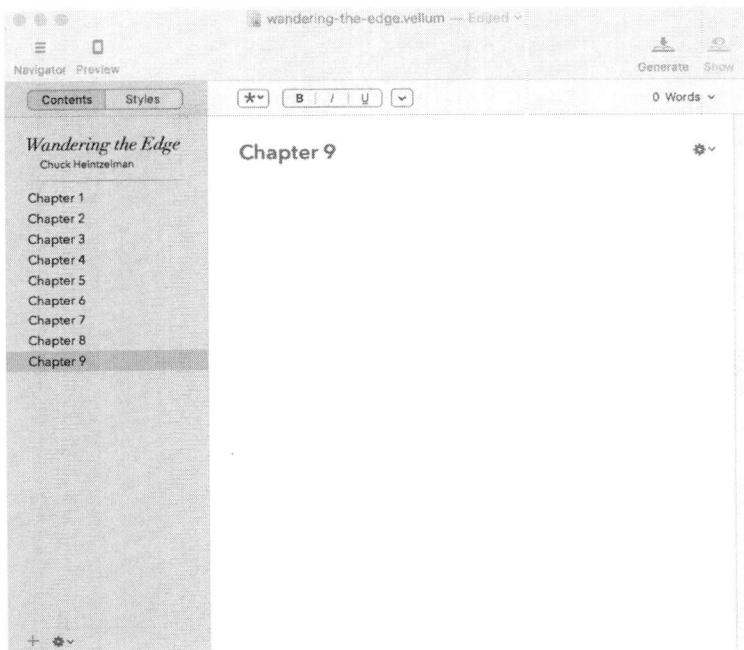

You'll notice when you have a chapter selected in the navigation pane (Chapter 9 in the above image), there's a small gear icon with a caret in the top right area of the chapter. If you click this, you can convert the Chapter to a different type of element.

I changed the element type of CHAPTER 1 to INTRODUCTION, then changed the next five chapters to VOLUMES. Finally, the skeleton was finished by converting the final three elements to ABOUT THE AUTHOR, ALSO BY, and COPYRIGHT elements.

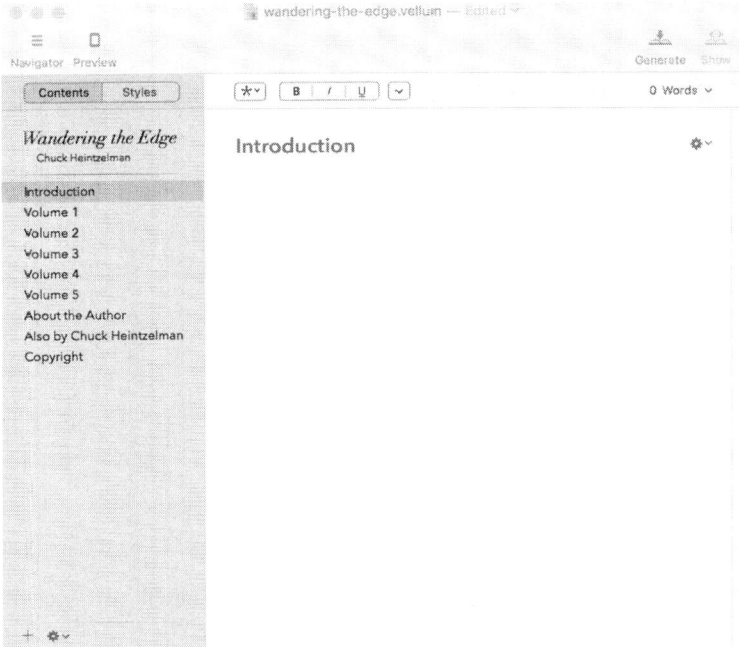

STEP 4 – ADD THE STORIES

For the next step, I wanted to populate each of the five Volumes with the stories. To do this, I found the .DOCX file with the story in Mac's Finder and dragged this file onto the top of the Volume (the VOLUME 1, VOLUME 2, etc.) in Vellum's Navigation pane. Then I renamed the Volume to the story title. The third short story didn't have chapter breaks, so I converted it back from a VOLUME to a CHAPTER.

After filling in the back matter and writing the Introduction, this short story collection is complete.

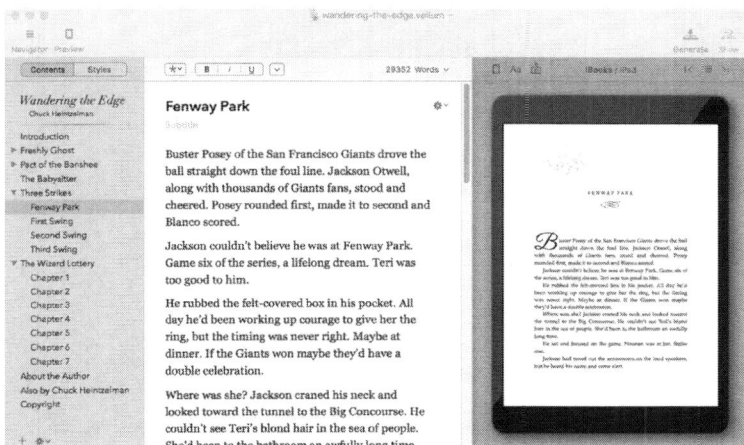

The above image shows the Vellum navigation pane on the left, with the entire structure of the book filled out. The center pane is the edit window, and on the right is the previewer.

❄

Yes, Vellum lets you preview what your ebook will look like on a variety of devices.

❄

How awesome is that?

You can easily compare what the iPhone experience is vs. the Kindle Paperwhite experience.

At the time of this writing, I'm using Vellum 1.3.9 and it provides previews for Apple iPhone, Apple iPad, Kindle Fire,

Kindle Paperwhite, Kobo Glo, Nook Simple Touch, and Android Tablet.

So far this tutorial has been quick and easy. There are only two steps left, and here is where the REAL FUN starts!

STEP 5 – TWEAKING THE STYLE

Vellum 1.3.9 has eight different styles, which allow you to add touches such as drop caps, ornamental breaks, and other flourishes.

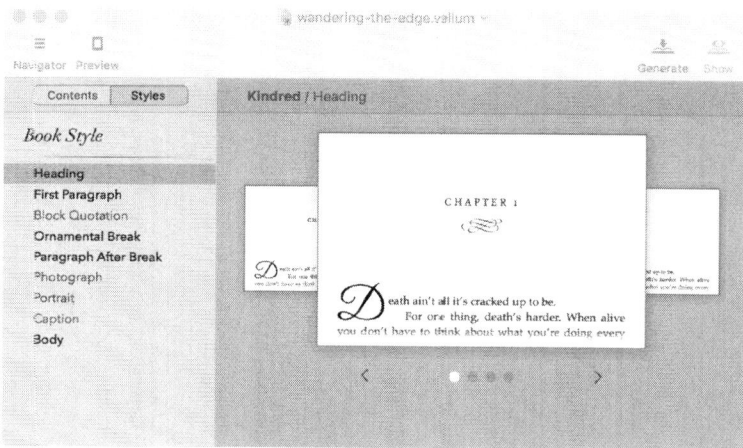

You can tweak the individual components of the style. Things such as the Heading, Block Quotations, and how Portraits are displayed.

When you pick a style here, the style is changed throughout the entire ebook.

STEP 6 – GENERATING THE EBOOKS

This is my favorite step: clicking which platforms I want and generating the ebooks.

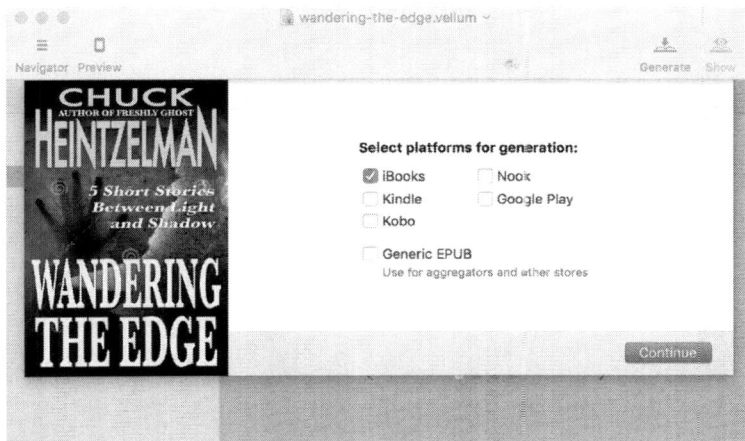

There's something magical about how the spinner spins as the ebooks are generated for each platform, knowing that in just a minute all the versions of my ebook will be finished and ready to upload to Kobo, Amazon, iBooks, and other storefronts.

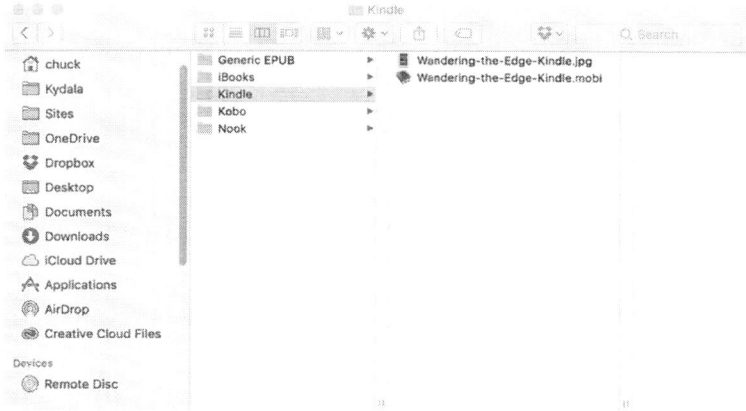

Vellum places each ebook and the cover image to use for the platform in separate folders.

❄

FROM START TO FINISH, THE ABOVE STEPS TAKE ABOUT 10 minutes.

I didn't cover a number of Vellum features; for example, *Store Links*. This feature allows you to specify separate links, which are specific to each store. In other words, an Amazon Store Link will only appear in the Kindle version of your ebook.

WHAT VELLUM CANNOT DO

Okay, here's the list of negative things I promised at the beginning of this chapter. (*These items pertain to the current version of Vellum, version 1.3.9.*)

- **No Access to HTML** – Being a techie, I like to access the code behind the ebook, tweaking things here and there. You cannot do this in Vellum.
- **No Tables** – With Vellum, you cannot have tables in your ebook. Tables aren't very important in fiction, but in nonfiction they're frequently used.
- **Incomplete Style Customization** – The styles in your ebook can only be what Vellum provides. Yes, there's a certain level of customization, but you cannot fully customize the style.
- **No Internal Links** – You cannot have text within your ebook link to another page. External links to websites are fine, but internal links aren't provided. Internal links are frequently used for footnotes.
- **Not Enough Hot Keys** – Vellum is designed to use the mouse or trackpad. I prefer using hot keys and had to set up many macros to achieve this.

So basically, if Vellum doesn't provide a feature through their menu system, you cannot do it.

Still, it is the best ebook creation software available today, so I've learned to work around any shortcomings.

CHAPTER FIVE
THE PROBLEMS WITH MULTI-AUTHOR BUNDLES

" Where large sums of money are concerned, it is advisable to trust nobody.

AGATHA CHRISTIE

THIS CHAPTER DISCUSSES THE PROBLEMS INHERENT WITH multi-author bundles.

THE MAIN PROBLEM

Building multi-author bundles is easy. We'll cover that in the next chapter. But before getting to that, I want to discuss the one, big, overriding problem with multi-author bundles:

HANDLING THE MONEY

- Who is going publish the bundle and track the sales and income?

- How long will the bundle be on sale?
- How will the bundle's income be divided among the authors?
- When will the income be disbursed?
- How will promotion costs (if any) be shared?

It's not a trivial task to handle the money, month after month, and communicate effectively with all the authors in the bundle.

YOU MUST HAVE A CONTRACT

Okay, here's the standard disclaimer: *I'm not a lawyer. I have no legal training whatsoever. This is not legal advice. Nothing in this entire book should be construed as legal advice.*

But as a businessperson, I would never participate in a multi-author bundle that does not have a contract that explicitly defines the five bullet points under HANDLING THE MONEY above.

Doing a multi-author bundle without a contract is a quick way to lose friends and get tangled up in unwanted lawsuits.

BUNDLING SERVICES ARE FIDUCIARIES

They have a legal obligation to act in the best interests of the authors in the bundle. Services such as BundleRabbit and Story-Bundle are entrusted with the care of the monies.

These services use contracts.

BundleRabbit, for instance, requires bundle participants to agree to the *BundleRabbit for Authors Publishing and Bundling Terms and Conditions*, which spells out exactly how royalties are divided and distributed.

And don't forget that ebook bundling services handle the publishing, delivery, sales, and customer support.

IT'S A BIT LIKE HAVING CO-AUTHORS

When you're in a bundle with other authors, it's a bit like co-authoring. You are creating a new product—the bundle—with the creative work of others.

Are you comfortable with that?

Do you want your name associated with everyone in the bundle?

And vice versa.

Just something to think about.

THINK OF PROMOTIONS DOWN THE ROAD

Another thing to think about is how the bundle may limit future promotions of your product.

Do you plan on doing a KDP Select with your book? If so, make sure the multi-author bundle you're in is for a limited time.

What about Nook First? Once your book has been bundled, you cannot participate in this program.

Or what about BookBub? Will participating in the bundle limit doing a BookBub on your book?

The point is, think about the long-term effect of being bundled and how it can limit future promotions with your book.

CHAPTER SIX
BUILDING MULTI-AUTHOR
BUNDLES

❝ It [Vellum] makes box sets REALLY easy.

JOANNA PENN, NEW YORK TIMES AND
USA TODAY BESTSELLING AUTHOR

THIS CHAPTER BUILDS ON CHAPTER FOUR – BUILDING A Single Author Bundle *with Vellum. It shows how quick and easy it is to build multi-author box sets.*

STEP 0 – PREP WORK

A cover image for the bundle needs to be created prior to creating the bundle. This is the image that will be part of the ebook and used to advertise the ebook at Kobo, Amazon, iBooks, etc.

But the main preparation work is to have each of the ebooks you're bundling available as Vellum files. Hopefully, each of the authors in the bundle use Vellum and can provide the Vellum file. If not, you'll need to have their ebook in .DOCX format and create a Vellum file from this .DOCX. (See help.vellum.pub/importing for details.)

Once you have each of the individual ebooks as Vellum files, the entire process takes about 10 minutes...including generating the platform-specific ebook files for the box set.

Building the bundle is largely a case of dragging and dropping files.

STEP 1 – THE BOOK INFO

The first step is to create a new file in Vellum and enter the book's information.

Since this bundle has multiple authors, each author name is added on this screen. The author names will appear on the bundle's title page automatically.

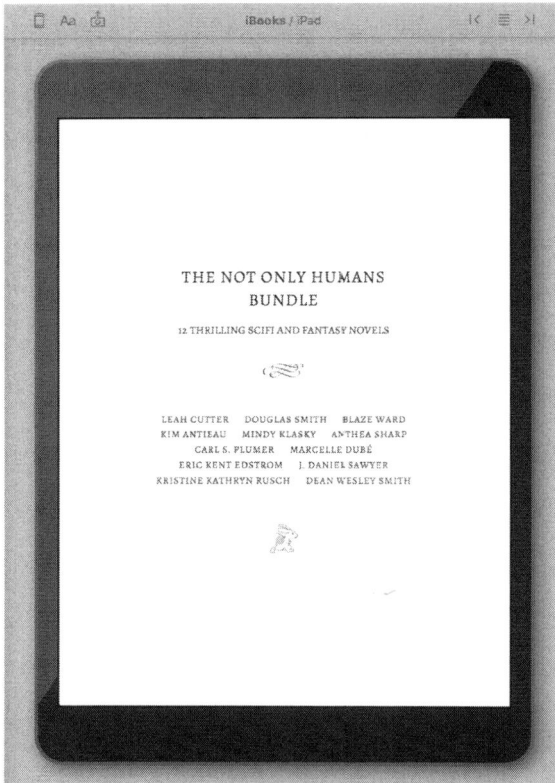

STEP 2 – THE COVER

This step is exactly the same as it was when building the single author bundle. Switch to the Cover tab and add the cover.

STEP 3 – CREATE THE EBOOK SKELETON

When creating the bundle's skeleton, create a bunch of blank chapters in the middle of the book. The reason for these extra chapters is because in the next step, when each book is dragged into the bundle, we want to drag the books in between two existing chapters (we'll get to that in a second.)

For now, create the skeleton with the extra chapters.

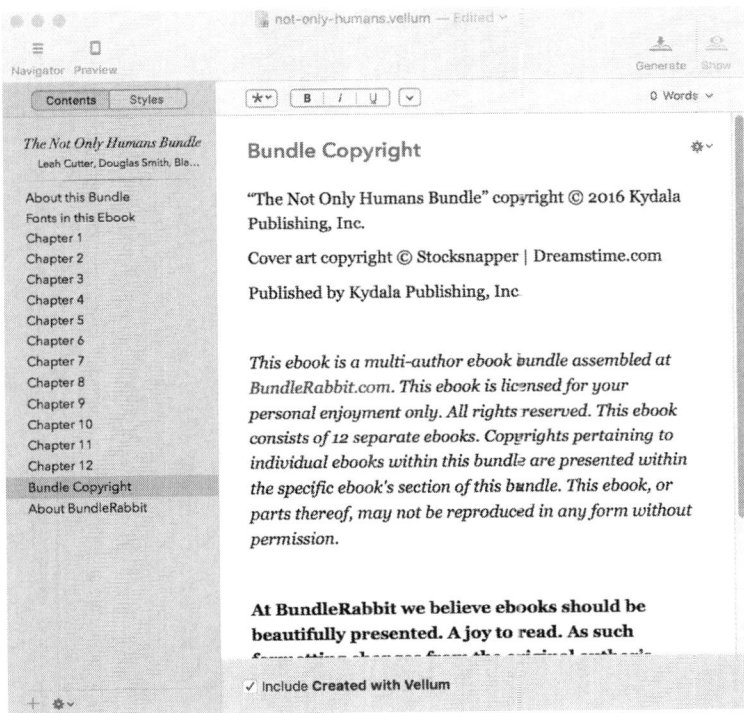

You may notice in the image above there's a Bundle Copyright page. Because each book we'll drag into this bundle will have its own copyright page, there's no need to display the copyright notice for the individual books. Still, I always add a Bundle Copyright page containing the copyright notice for the form of the bundle itself and the cover image.

STEP 4 – DRAG THE VELLUM FILES INTO THE BUNDLE

Next, drag each of the Vellum files created or obtained during the prep work into the bundle.

Drop these files into Vellum's navigation page BETWEEN two chapters. Doing it this way ensures the dragged file is positioned correctly.

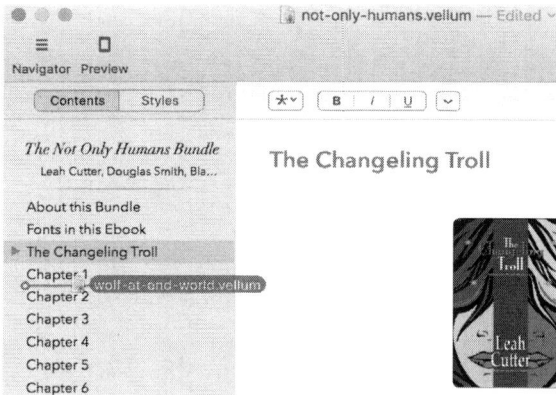

When you drop the file, Vellum will ask you whether to want to use the book cover for the new Volume.

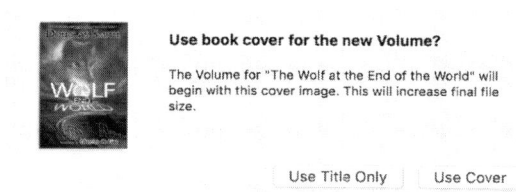

If you are worried about the final size of the final bundle, use the title only. This will create a title page for the volume in the book. Otherwise the cover will appear at the beginning of the volume.

✳

NOTE

In Vellum 1.3.9 I could find no way to change this "Use Cover?" decision. So if you decide to use covers and then change your mind, you'll need to delete the volume from the bundle and re-drag and drop the Vellum files again, answering the question differently the second time.

✳

AFTER DROPPING THE VELLUM FILE INTO THE BUNDLE AND answering the "Use Cover?" question, click on the gear icon next to the Volume's title in Vellum's edit pane. Choose Add Author and then type in the author's name.

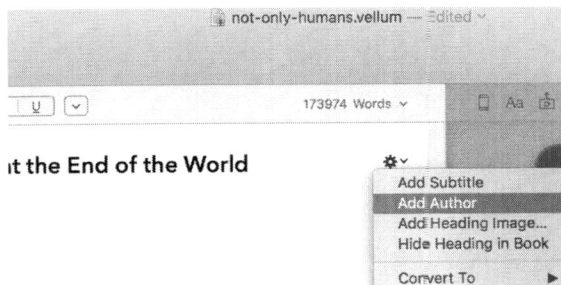

STEP 5 – REMOVE EXTRA CHAPTERS

Once all the volumes have been added to your bundle, go back and delete all those placeholder chapters between the volumes.

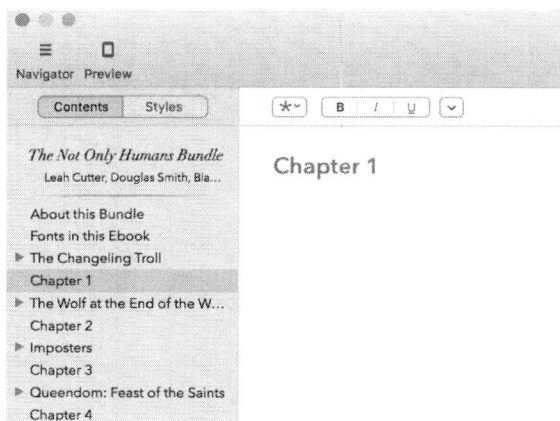

STEP 6 – CHECK THE TABLE OF CONTENTS

Before wrapping up the bundle, view the bundle's table of contents in Vellum's preview pane.

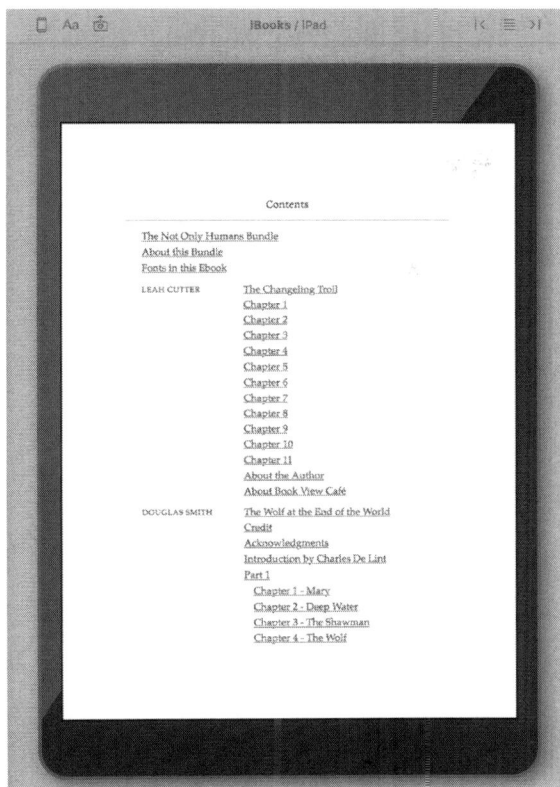

Here you can double-check that each of the author's names were typed correctly, all the extra place-holder chapters were removed, and everything looks good.

STEP 7 – WRAPPING UP

To finish up the bundle, perform the same last two steps as detailed in *Chapter 4 – Building a Single Author Bundle*.

- **Step 5 – Tweaking the Style**. The style you set

within Vellum applies across the entire bundle, including each volume within the bundle. Readers will have a consistent experience throughout.

- **Step 6 – Generating the Ebooks**. Bam! One click and you're ready to upload the bundle to Kobo, Amazon, iBooks, etc.

❄

I'M REALLY NOT SURE HOW THIS PROCESS COULD BE ANY easier.

CHAPTER SEVEN
DELIVERING BUNDLES TO CUSTOMERS

66 I've been blown away by how good it [BookFunnel] is.

MARK DAWSON, BESTSELLING AUTHOR

THIS CHAPTER EXPLORES THE VARIOUS WAYS OF DELIVERING bundles to your readers.

EBOOK PUBLISHERS

When you sell your bundle through Amazon, Amazon handles delivering the bundle to the customer's Kindle. Same goes for iBooks, Kobo, and any of the major publishers.

This is the optimal delivery method. The reader is already accustomed to receiving ebooks from their favorite vendor. They should be comfortable with the process.

And, best of all, you do not have to provide technical support to your readers. You don't have to explain to them how to *sideload* ebooks into their device. You don't have to troubleshoot problems when their ebooks don't load.

❄

DEFINITION OF *SIDELOAD*

This is a term similar to *upload* and *download*, referring to how data is transferred between two devices. With ebooks, this means loading the ebook onto the ebook reader from your computer.

❄

YOUR WEBSITE

When you sell ebook bundles from your website, the most common technique is to upload the bundle to your server (uploading both .EPUB and .MOBI formats) and then provide your customer with a private link to download the ebook.

And then, of course, explain to your customer how to sideload the bundle onto their reader.

If you have a Wordpress website, there are a number of plugins to help you manage the uploaded files. But even with these plugins, there's still the issue of sideloading.

Unless you use a service such as BookFunnel.

BOOKFUNNEL

This is an amazing and reasonably priced service that helps you deliver ebooks to your customers.

With BookFunnel, you upload your ebook's cover, the .EPUB, and the .MOBI. Then you create a link for delivering the ebook.

When the customer goes to the link, they see a page showcasing your book with a big, fat "Get My Book" button.

When the customer clicks the button, they get a list of choices, allowing them to pick the device they like to read on.

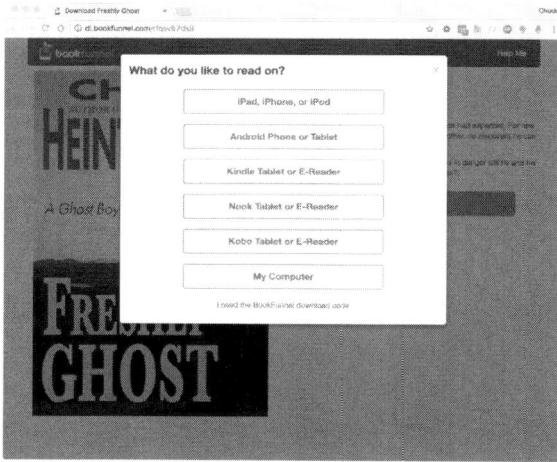

When the customer picks their device, they may get another screen asking the specific model of the device.

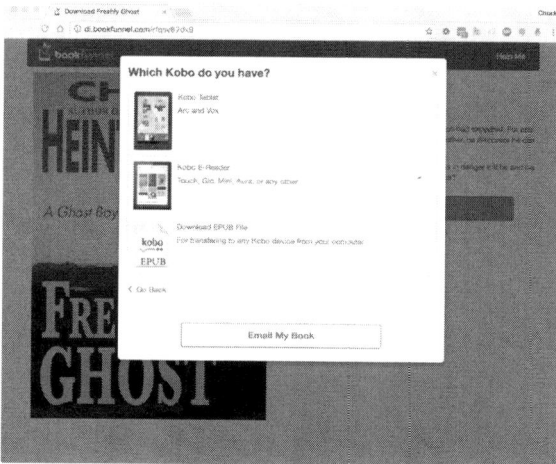

Finally, they'll receive the specific instructions for getting your ebook onto their device.

Best of all, if the customer has any problems, BookFunnel handles the customer support.

Check out bookfunnel.com for more details.

BUNDLING SERVICES

When your ebook bundle is sold through services such as BundleRabbit or StoryBundle, the customer goes to a download page to download their ebooks. This download page lists all the ebooks within the bundle individually and allows the customer to download them one by one and sideload them into their device.

These services also provide a *Send to Kindle* feature, which emails individual ebooks to the customer's kindle.

BundleRabbit also allows the customer to download the Box Set version of the bundle, which is the entire bundle as one multi-volume .EPUB or .MOBI.

The bundling service handles any technical support with the customer.

❄

EXCITING NEWS!

As of January 2017, BundleRabbit has partnered with BookFunnel to deliver books through their funnel. Customers still have a download page at BundleRabbit, but when they click on the ebook they want (or the entire box set), it takes them to the BookFunnel page to select their device and the specific instructions to download it.

❄

CHAPTER EIGHT
TYPES OF READERS

> Many authors—and I was no different here—don't have a clue about pricing. They think of one formula: *Low Price = More Sales.* Sometimes that's true, sometimes not. It depends on many factors, one being the type of reader. For example, to some readers a higher price indicates a higher quality book.
>
> A LITTLE ABOUT PRICING

THIS CHAPTER BREAKS DOWN READERS INTO DIFFERENT categories.

READER TYPE HELPS DETERMINE THE RETAIL PRICE

Pricing is a key variable in economic theories, financial modeling, and marketing. It's such an in-depth topic I recommend you research it on your own. If you search for books on "pricing" at

Amazon, there are more than 10,000 results. Even narrowing the search down to "retail pricing" shows 123 results at the time of this writing.

❄

HERE'S SOMETHING INTERESTING

Currently, the number one result on Amazon for "pricing" is The Strategy and Tactics of Pricing: New International Edition. *The Kindle edition of this book is currently priced at $103.96 and the hardcover edition is $74.50. With this pricing strategy, they're obviously pushing the hardcover.*

❄

KEEP IN MIND THAT PRICING THEORIES HAVE BEEN AROUND for hundreds of years. Even in this digital age, the strategies haven't changed.

Before hitting the next chapter and discussing pricing in more detail, I want to go over types of readers.

(*I first learned these particular breakdowns of reader types during the 2015 Publishing Master Class on the Oregon Coast, taught by Kristine Kathryn Rusch and Dean Wesley Smith.*)

TYPES OF READERS

- **TRUE FAN** – A True Fan will purchase everything

you produce without considering the price. They'll buy books, T-shirts, and pretty much anything related to the author.

- **LONG-TIME FAN** – A Long-Time Fan will purchase your work when they're ready for it. They've bought your work for years, sometimes decades. When they need something to read, and if they come across your work, they'll buy it. Price isn't a major consideration.

- **SOMETIMES FAN** – This is a fan that likes some of your work, but doesn't care for some of it. They're fans loyal to certain genres or series you write. People who love Nora Roberts but don't care for J.D. Robb (her pseudonym) are Sometimes Fans. Price is a consideration, but your brand in the area they love is the most important thing to the Sometimes Fan.

- **GENRE FAN** – When these readers finish a book, they'll first look for something by the same author in the genre. Or they'll look for their favorite author in the genre. If they can't find anything, they'll pick up something similar. Price can be a consideration (we'll get to that in a moment).

- **VORACIOUS READERS** – These people constantly buy books or get books from the library. They're always reading. As with the Genre Fan, the price can be an important consideration.

- **OCCASIONAL READERS** – These people like to read and they may have been Voracious Readers in the past, but right now, because of their job or family, they only occasionally read. The importance of pricing can vary widely with these readers.

- **LIKES TO READ** – These people are Occasional Readers who enjoy reading, but may only read one book a year. Or they may read one book a month. It all depends on their life circumstances.
- **NON-READERS** – Believe it or not, non-readers do buy books. They give books to others, but they don't care to read themselves. Like the later categories of readers, the importance of pricing varies wildly for non-readers.

Other than True Fan and Long-Time Fans, the type of reader doesn't help much when determining pricing. Let's break down the readers a different way. These categories below are based on how the reader buys.

HOW A READER BUYS

- **ALWAYS BUYS NEW** – These readers always want the best, new books. If there's a hardcover available, they'll pick it up. Or they'll pick up the book for their digital library. Price to these readers isn't as important as having the best.
- **SOMETIMES BUYS NEW** – These readers will buy new when they see it, but they'll also buy used if they see a used book they think they'll like. Price usually is secondary to getting the book they want right now.

- **ALWAYS BUYS DISCOUNTED** – These readers either cannot pay full price because of their financial situation or their preference is to *always get the deal*. Pricing is very important here.
- **ALWAYS GETS FREE BOOKS** – These readers are similar to the discount buyers. They don't buy books at all. If it's because they don't have the money, then these readers can slide up the scale to buying discounted or buying new. Or not. A small percentage of the people will never pay for ebooks. The price of $0.00 is the most important consideration here.

Nobody falls 100% within any of the above categories. One reader may be a True Fan of Neil Gaiman and a Voracious Reader who likes to buy discounted but will sometimes buy new. Another may love the Urban Fantasy genre and always buy new when possible.

So a person can be a different type of reader depending on the author or genre they're reading.

The point of all this is to know your customer, the reader. And further, to know how your pricing targets different types of readers.

> If you're not worried that you're pricing it too cheap, you're not pricing it cheap enough.

ROY H. WILLIAMS, BEST-SELLING
AUTHOR AND MARKETING
CONSULTANT.

> Cutting prices or putting things on sale is not a sustainable business strategy.

HOWARD SCHULTZ, CEO STARBUCKS

As I mentioned in the last chapter, pricing is a vast and complicated subject. So much so that pricing is a major area of study. Whatever pricing strategy you come up with, it's guaranteed somebody will disagree with it.

So this chapter is NOT an absolute bible on pricing bundles. No.

I'm simply going to share a few things to think about when it comes to pricing and marketing bundles.

A SURPRISING CHART

I recently attended a publishing conference on the Oregon coast and one of the speakers there was Mark Lefebvre, Director of Self-Publishing & Author Relations at Kobo.com.

Mark presented an interesting column chart on pricing that really caught my eye. He kindly provided the chart for publication in this book.

Actual Price Volumes at Kobo – Year 2016

All books, ALL Genres, all prices normalized to USD

This chart shows the number of titles available at various prices, starting with $0.99 on the left and moving toward $21+ on the right.

What really caught my eye was that column on the far right, the over-$21 column.

When I asked Mark what types of ebooks were in that over-$21 column, he replied they were mostly box sets.

Interesting.

HOW TO DETERMINE YOUR BUNDLE'S RETAIL PRICE

Look at your competition. What are similar bundles in the same genre selling at? How well are they selling?

But just because you've noticed hundreds of romance bundles setting at 99 cents, that doesn't mean that's the best price for your romance bundle.

There's no easy one-size-fits-all answer to pricing. It all depends on the value of your bundle and the types of readers you're targeting. Are you going after the Always Buys Discounted Readers? Or will your bundle appeal to the Long-Time Fan or Genre Fan?

Let's say you've priced your bundle at 99 cents. The math works out that you'll make about $35 when you sell 100 copies. But if your bundle is priced at $2.99, you only need to sell about 17 copies to make the same income.

And you need only 5 sales to make the same if the bundle's priced at $9.99.

WHEN DETERMINING YOUR BUNDLE'S PRICE, FOLLOW A simple, two-step process:

1. Determine a retail price for the bundle.

2. Track your sales numbers over time for this price.

In other words, test. Yes, testing is the big secret. When pricing, you must:

TEST, TEST, and TEST again.

Don't perform your price testing over a few days. At a minimum, test across a full week. Better yet, use month-long tests.

And always be mindful of other factors that can affect sales over the course of a test. Was there a holiday? Did one of your blog posts go viral?

Ideally when testing, test only a single thing. In this case, the price.

ONE PRICING STRATEGY

Here's one strategy when pricing bundles.

- Add up the retail price of all the books in the bundle.
- Apply a discount, such as 30% off.
- Round up or down to the nearest 99 cents.

So if you're pricing a trilogy and your first book is available at 99 cents, but the next two books cost $5.99 each, that's a total of $12.97 if the books are bought individually. At 30% off, rounded up to the nearest 99 cents, the trilogy price could be $9.99.

A bundle of 6 novels, retailing at $5.99 each, would be $24.99

using this strategy. Does that seem too high? You could go lower. At 40% off, this formula would make the price $21.99.

If that still seems high to you, remember the customer is still getting a deal. And remember, once you have a standard retail price for the bundle, you can still have an occasional sale on the bundle.

For 3 days only,
6 books for $11.99.
Less than 2 bucks each.
Over 75% off retail.

Of course, you'll still want to do some price testing when using this strategy.

PRICING IN FOREIGN MARKETS

Kobo and Amazon allow you set the price your ebook sells at in foreign markets. Apple allows you do to this as well, but there are more than 50 stores you can set the price in. I tend not to set all those individual prices with Apple and just go with the defaults. (I explain why at the very end of this book.)

Elsewhere, you should set the prices in foreign markets. You can do this at Apple as well if you want to take the time.

If you don't adjust the price for foreign markets, at best you're leaving money on the table. At worst, you're pricing your bundle out of sales.

Here's a list of currencies and suggested pricing strategies. *Keep in mind currency rates change all the time, thus these strategies need to be tweaked over time.*

- **Australian dollars** (AUD) – Round the converted currency up to the nearest 99 cents. For instance, $9.99 USD is currently $13.28 AUD, so round this to $13.99 AUD.
- **Brazilian reals** (BRL) – Round up to nearest 99 cents; i.e. 32,43 BRL becomes 32,99 BRL.
- **British pounds** (GBP) – Round down to nearest 49 or 99 cents.
- **Canadian dollars** (CAD) – Round up to nearest 99 cents.
- **Euros** (EUR) – Round down to the nearest 99 cents.
- **Hong Kong dollars** (HKD) – Round up to the nearest 99 cents.
- **Indian rupees** (INR) – Divide by 5 and round to nearest 99. Products are so cheap in India you have to cut the price to sell anything.
- **Mexican pesos** (MXN) – Round up to the nearest 99 cents.
- **New Zealand dollars** (NZD) – Round up to the nearest 99 cents.
- **Philippine pesos** (PHP) – Round up to the nearest 99 cents.
- **South African rand** (ZAR) – Divide by 3 and round to nearest 99 cents. South Africa is an emerging English-reading market and I really want my bundles to sell there.

- **Swiss francs** (CHF) – Round up to nearest 99 cents.
- **Turkish lira** (TRY) – Round up to nearest 99 cents.

Anything not in the list above, such as the Japanese yen or Taiwan dollars, I just keep at whatever the suggested conversion is.

A QUICK LIST OF MARKETING IDEAS

Here are a few marketing ideas for selling your bundles.

- **Newsletters** – Email your subscribers when new bundles come available or a bundle goes on sale for a limited period of time.
- **Newsletter Giveaways** – Give a free copy of your *Sampler Bundle* to new newsletter subscribers.
- **Blog Posts** – Write a blog post about the bundle when it's released. If it's a multi-author bundle, write a post each day focusing on a different author and book in the bundle.
- **Goodreads** – Add the bundle to Goodreads.
- **Facebook Posts** – Create posts when new bundles come available or a bundle goes on sale for a limited period of time.
- **Facebook Contests** – Give the bundle away in random drawings for people who share your posts.
- **Facebook Pages** – Create a page for the bundle on Facebook.
- **Twitter Tweets** – Tweet when new bundles come

available or a bundle goes on sale for a limited period of time.

- **Twitter Contests** – Give the bundle away in random drawings for people who retweet your tweet.

There are many more ways to market your bundles. This list just scratches the surface. Be creative.

CHAPTER TEN
BOX SET IMAGES

" Writers aren't in competition with one another. It isn't a zero sum game. If you have a good book, a good cover...you can sell well.

J. A. KONRATH, BEST-SELLING AUTHOR
AND SELF-PUBLISHING ADVOCATE

THIS CHAPTER EXPLORES THE TWO TYPES OF COVERS USED FOR bundles: 2D covers and 3D covers. Which type should be used where? Also, some cover creation resources are provided.

2D COVERS

A 2D Cover for a box set is exactly what it sounds like: a 2-dimensional cover image for the ebook file. There are a few different styles you can use for 2D covers.

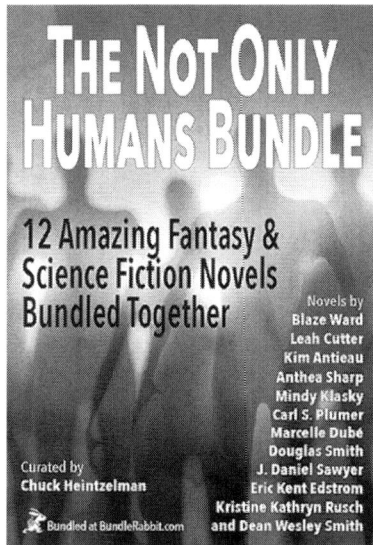

Anthology Style Cover

This above cover is from a bundle I curated. It looks kind of like an anthology cover with the authors listed on the front. Personally, this is my favorite style of cover. It works well for multi-author bundles.

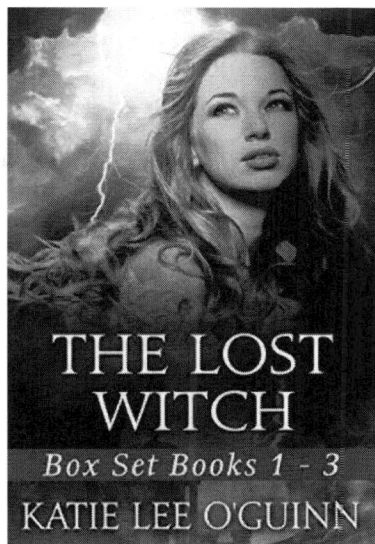

Single Image Cover

This type of cover has a single image, but designates it as a box set. This is a very clean way to go.

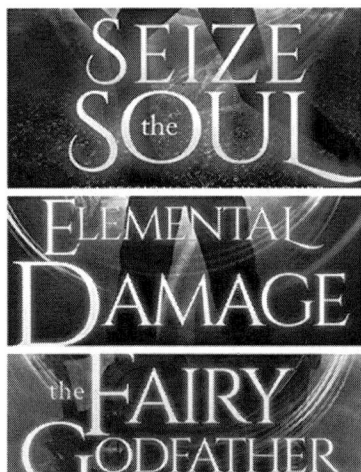

A collage cover

This style uses a collage of covers to create the box set cover. Sometimes these can be very striking, especially if the entire series in the box set is branded well.

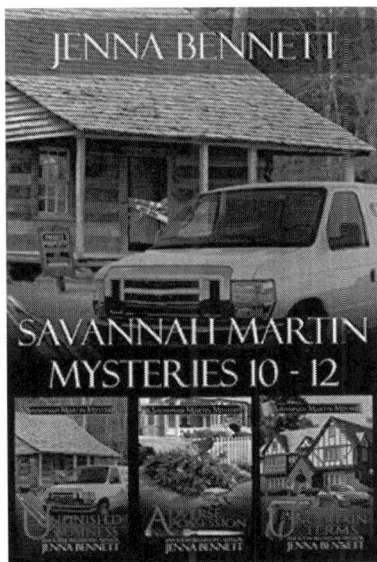

Cover with 2D covers in it

This style of cover uses 2D covers of the titles in the box set within the cover. The background can be an image, design, or even just gradient colors. Although popular, I personally don't care for this style of box set cover for the simple fact that at thumbnail size, the individual covers are impossible to read.

Cover with 3D covers on it

Just like the previous example, but using 3D covers instead of 2D covers. And just like the 2D example, the individual covers are impossible to read at thumbnail size.

A GREAT RESOURCE FOR CREATING 3D COVERS

If you use Photoshop, a great resource for creating 3D covers for a single book is psdcovers.com.

Using their mockups, you can convert your 2D cover image into 3D Versions of:

- Paperbacks
- Spray cans

- Hardbound books
- Containers
- Paper bags
- Tin cans
- Paint cans
- Business cards
- And more

They have dozens and dozens of mockups.

Often I'll use their upright, paperback, spine-facing-in mockup to create a fan of all the books in a bundle.

I call this type of image a *Cover Fan*. This type of artwork can be used in other images for advertising.

3D BOX SET COVERS

With 3D box set covers, you can have the spines showing either on the left or the right.

Spines on the left

Spines on the right.

You can also have individual spines showing like in the first example. Or you can have a single piece of artwork covering all the spines as in the second example.

Personally, I like having individual spines. It's a bit more work to create, but focus here is on the bundle as a collection of individual items. Still, perhaps you're creating a themed bundle and want the emphasis on a common theme. By using a single piece of art across all the books, you place a greater focus on the commonality of the books.

WHEN TO USE 3D COVERS

Only use 3D as part of ads, or in posts on your blog or Facebook. You can also use the 3D Cover within a 2D Cover, similar to the last example of 2D Covers above, but using a box set image instead of individual 3D book images.

Never use the 3D image as the box set cover on Kobo, Amazon, iBooks, or other outside vendors. Use 2D Covers at these sites.

Let me repeat that...

NEVER USE 3D COVER IMAGES ON OUTSIDE VENDORS

There are two reasons for this.

First, some vendors (such as iBooks) do not accept 3D covers. They fear that a customer will see a 3D image and expect to get a physical box set, not an electronic version.

The second reason is the space that Kobo, Amazon, etc., allocate to display an ebook's cover is optimized for single books, not box sets. The 3D image will be smaller and there will be wasted white space.

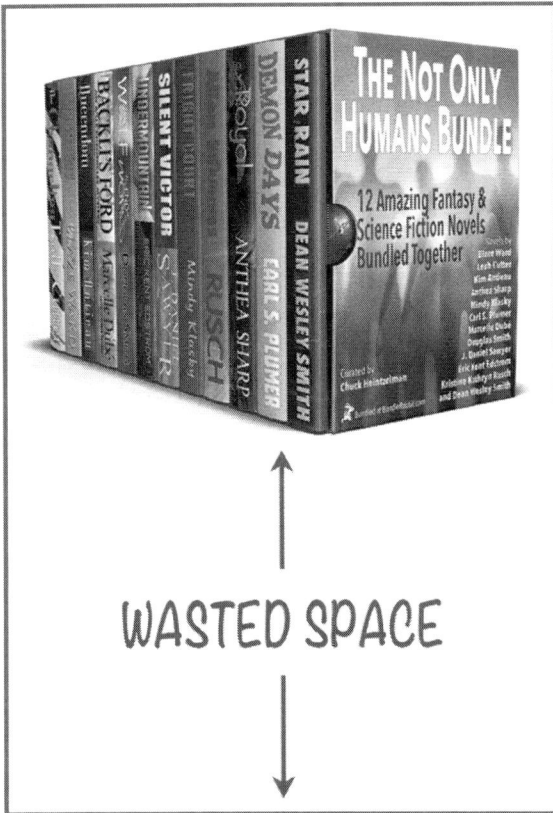

WASTED SPACE

As you can see, you lose almost half of your cover space.

❄

MANY PEOPLE USE 3D BOX SET IMAGES

Yes, if you search on your favorite ebook retailer for box sets, you'll see hundreds of examples where 3D Box Set images are used.

DON'T DO IT.

You want your box set to stand out from this crowd, don't you?

❄

RESOURCES FOR CREATING 3D IMAGES

Here are a few resources that can help you when creating 3D box set images.

- fiverr – If you don't want to do the work yourself, you can hire it done for a reasonable price. Search for "box set" or "book cover design" at fiverr and find a cover design artist. I haven't used fiverr for a 3D Cover, but have used it for other projects and have always been satisfied.
- CoverVault – This site provides tutorials and Photoshop mockups. They do have some free mockups. They also have box set templates available for purchase. Their templates are easy to use even with basic Photoshop knowledge. (I use their Boxset Bundle Vol. 1 to create 3D Box Set Images at BundleRabbit.)
- YouTube – Search for "3d box set" and you'll find a number of tutorials.
- Dreamstime, Shutterstock, iStockPhoto, or your favorite stock photo site – Search for "3d boxset cover" and you'll often be able to find blank box set images you can use as the base of your image. If you're skilled

with Photoshop, Gimp, or another image editor, this can be a good choice.

> Nashville has a great creative atmosphere. It's a small, close-knit music community that you can't find anywhere else.

KIM CARNES, TWO-T ME GRAMMY
AWARD–WINNING SINGER-
SONGWRITER.

COMMUNICATION AS COMMUNITY

THERE'S ONE ASPECT OF PARTICIPATING IN A MULTI-author bundle that few people realize. It is the communication between the authors participating in the bundle. I like to think of this as a mini-community. Yes, this mini-community is often short-lived, only through the life of the bundle, but it is there.

And like the quote at the top of this chapter, this is a community that doesn't exist anywhere else.

Every bundle has a different level of this mini-community, from no community at all to a real feeling of fellowship arising from shared goals and actions. It all comes down to how well the authors communicate with each other. I've seen bundles on both sides of the spectrum. Bundles with little-to-no communication have zero community. They also don't sell as well as bundles with better communication.

COMMUNICATION METHODS

The easiest and most common method of communication in a bundle is a group email. The bundle's curator sends a group email welcoming everyone to the bundle, encouraging authors to communicate their activities with the bundle. It just builds from there as authors get involved.

Here are a few other methods of communication.

- **Friending in Facebook**. Everyone in the bundle should friend each other. Whenever someone posts about the bundle, everyone should help boost the signal by sharing the posts.
- **Facebook Pages** – Sometimes the curator will set up a page just for the bundle.
- **Google Docs** – Curators can set up shared documents and spreadsheets with important dates and marketing information about the bundle.
- **Twitter Follows** – Like with Facebook, every author in the bundle should follow each other and retweet bundle-related posts.

- **Twitter Hashtags** – Use hashtags for bundle-related posts.
- **Message Boards** – You can even participate in bundle-related message boards to share ideas and files. (BundleRabbit provides bundle specific message boards.)

WHAT TO COMMUNICATE

This list is not exhaustive. Use this list as a springboard for ideas.

- **Ad Artwork** – Share the artwork used for ads with other authors in the bundle.
- **Newsletter Announcements** – Tell the other authors before you share the bundle in your newsletter. This way they can sign up for your newsletter and see what you say about the bundle.
- **Blog Posts** – Many blog posts can be generated from the bundle. There's the announcement of the bundle. But what about spotlighting the individual authors in the bundle? Or the individual ebooks? Whenever you create bundle-related blog posts, share this with the group.
- **Facebook Posts** – Same deal as blog posts.
- **Author Promotions** – Is an author doing some sort of additional promotion? Something like a BOGO (buy-one, get-one-free) with one of their own stories? Communicate this.
- **Outside Promotions** – Is the bundle part of

promotion outside the authors' own efforts? A themed blog post from someone not directly participating in the bundle? A Kobo promotion? This should always be communicated with the authors in the bundle.

- **Feedback** – Share positive feedback you've heard about the bundle with the bundle's participants.
- **Ideas** – Share other ideas about the bundle.

WHY COMMUNICATION IS IMPORTANT

Not only does the bundle sell better when the authors are excited and share this excitement, but it's also a great way to build friendships.

NETWORKING FOR INTROVERTS

Everybody knows that writers are often introverts. (The same could be said of computer programmers and since I fall in both categories, I have a double-whammy here.) Although introverted, writers are warm people and welcoming to other writers. Yeah, there are exceptions, but for the most part writers enjoy the company of other writers.

After all, we writers share a common obsession.

When you look at the authors in a bundle as a mini-community, it's a perfect, low-key way to make new connections.

That is, as long as you actually participate in the conversations and aren't a Lurker Louie (or Lucy) sitting in the background, maybe with the lights down low, quietly reading all the messages, while slowly petting your hairless cat. (Hey, I like cats. If you have a hairless one, you're free to pet it as long as you're participating in the conversation.)

The point I'm making here is that even if it's outside your comfort zone, when you're in a bundle with other writers, force yourself to communicate. To ask questions. To share thoughts and ideas about the bundle.

You may make a connection that lasts a lifetime.

> Discoverability, in marketing, refers to a style of marketing that aims to help potential customers find a product or service when they need it, rather than being force-fed advertising messages at unwelcome times. Discoverable marketing has emerged as a more passive approach to internet marketing than traditional ads.
>
> DEFINITION OF DISCOVERABILITY FROM TECHNONPEDIA

DISCOVERABILITY IS A MASSIVE TOPIC. IN THIS CHAPTER WE'LL define what it is, present a few techniques, and focus on how bundling increases discoverability.

INTERRUPTION MARKETING

Let's start with defining the opposite of discoverability, Interruption Marketing. Old-style marketing is all about interruptions. Radio or TV ads interrupt the program with advertisements. Telemarketing calls interrupt your day. Mail or even email campaigns interrupt your normal flow when checking mail. Those transitional online ads that put an ad in front of your face before you can see the content you want to see are a big interruption.

It's all about stopping people and forcing them to pay attention or deal the marketing message in some way.

With the internet, discoverability is more effective and less off-putting to people.

WHAT IS DISCOVERABILITY?

The quote at top of this chapter defines discoverability, but let's get really clear here about what's being discovered.

❄

DISCOVERABILITY IS ALL ABOUT BEING FOUND.

But the focus here is not necessarily your book being found, but the breadcrumbs leading to your book being found.

❄

YES, PART OF DISCOVERABILITY IS WHEN A READER

searches for you or your book in a search engine. That's a large part. But another part is all the links everywhere leading to your book or web page. These links, by the way, also help with the search engine part.

In other words, you must have links going to your content. And you must have great content.

Discoverability comes from:

- **Search engines**. Google, Bing, and Yahoo.
- **Pay per click (PPC) advertising.** Yes, PPC advertising does increase your discoverability. It's not the ad-in-your-face type marketing. PPC ads only appear on relevant search result pages (SERP).
- **Social media.** Facebook, Twitter, and Google+.
- **Content marketing.** This is not pitching your ebooks, but having useful and relevant content that lead potential customers to your ebooks.
- **Communities.** LibraryThing, Goodreads, MobileRead, and other Internet communities.

THE "ARTISTS" AND FIELD OF DREAMS

There are two attitudes I want to dispel. The first is the *I'm an artist and cannot sully myself with marketing* concept.

Okay, fine. I get that. I really do. But "artists" (*I have to put quotes around this*) who think this way are thinking of the old style, interruption marketing. Artist integrity is important, and part of this integrity should be sharing your work with the world. On the Internet, this sharing can be totally passive, but you have to do the basic work.

The second attitude is the *If I build it they will come* type thinking. This line comes from the movie *Field of Dreams*. I often suffer from this delusion. Sure, there's the occasional lightning strike that requires absolutely no marketing effort, yet your work goes viral. But should you base your business on chance?

If you have either of these attitudes and don't do the most basic, low-key marketing to increase your discoverability, in my opinion you're being a mook.

THE ULTRA-COMPETITIVE WORLD OF SEO

Search Engine Optimization (SEO) is all about obtaining high-ranking placements in the search engine results on Google, Bing, Yahoo, and other search engines.

It is probably the most competitive area of marketing on the Internet.

Still, there are a number of basic things you can do to help with your SEO.

DOUBLE-CHECK YOUR TITLE, DESCRIPTION, AND KEYWORDS

Make sure your book's description is good. Make sure you have clear keywords about your book.

MAKE SURE EVERYTHING IN YOUR CONTROL HAS LINKS BACK TO YOUR SITE

Clear out your browser's cookies and search for your name or book on Google. Do you have a partially set up Author Central page on Amazon? Fix it. Do you only have the first book in your series on Goodreads? Or on LibraryThing? Then get these updated. Make sure all your blogs, social media, and user profiles are up to snuff and have links to your web page. This includes EVERYTHING you can control.

USE GOOGLE ANALYTICS

You need to know how many visitors found your page, where they came from, and what search terms they've used. If you haven't set up a Google Analytics account and added the code to your website, do it.

LINK TO HIGH-QUALITY SITES

When adding content to your blog, link to other people's content. Today's search engine algorithms are sophisticated enough that they look at the quality of sites you link to and increase your weight accordingly.

USE GOOGLE+

This an item on my personal to do list. Yes. I have a Google+ account but haven't used it much at the time of this writing. But research tells me that using Google+ daily, doing the +1 thing on other's content, and building your circles will *increase your own results* at Google.

CLAIM YOUR BOOKS AND BUNDLES ON AMAZON

If your name isn't tied to every book or bundle available at Amazon, then claim it. Do this by going to your Author Central Books tab and clicking on ADD MORE BOOKS. Fill out the form and within a few days the book should appear in your bibliography at Author Central.

STRUCTURE YOUR BLOG POSTS FOR SEO

If you use Wordpress, install *Yoast SEO*. This helps you write well-formed, SEO posts. Follow these tips:

1. Use keywords in the page and title and headings.
2. Add keywords in the first 50 to 100 words of copy.
3. Use appropriate categories and tags for your post.
4. Use keywords in outgoing links ("Buy Gummi Worms" instead of "click here").
5. Have lots of unique, fresh copy.

BUILD LINKS TO YOUR SITE

Another way search engines weight your search engine results is the number and quality of links to your site. Here's a few ways to increase the links back to your site.

- Guest post on other blogs.

- Add links on social networks.
- Provide testimonials to others (with a link back to your site).
- Negotiate reciprocal links with fellow bloggers.
- Comment where appropriate on other sites (with a link back to your site).

❄

IT'S ALL ABOUT SPREADING YOUR BREADCRUMBS

You don't know how a reader will find you. It might be a link to a link to a link to your site. As you spread more breadcrumbs, the number of ways readers can find you goes up exponentially because it's not just the links you spread, but also the links others spread to where you're linked.

❄

HOW BUNDLES HELP DISCOVERABILITY

We've already mentioned the cross-pollination effect of multi-author bundles, but all bundles help with discoverability in other ways.

A bundle is another one of your products, linked everywhere your products are linked. Social media and blog posts about the bundle provide that second-level breadcrumb (the link to a link).

When you have more books under your name at retailers (such as Kobo and Amazon), you have more of the "Customer also bought..." links.

And the bundle itself, being an ebook, should have links to your web page (About the Author), your newsletter, and your other ebooks.

❄

MAKE DISCOVERABILITY A GAME

Imagine an old-time fulcrum scale with the left bucket weighed down by the success you want to achieve (whatever that is) and the right bucket weighed by your discoverability. Each time you add a new book or links to your books in the right bucket, it moves a little.

Problem is, you don't know how many books or links it will take for the success bucket to move all the way up.

So just keep on filling that right bucket. Eventually, you'll bring up the success bucket all the way to the top. That's when you redefine success and weigh that bucket back down again.

PART TWO

BUNDLING AT BUNDLERABBIT

Note: The BundleRabbit software described in this section is for BundleRabbit 2.0, which is scheduled to be released January 2017.

CHAPTER THIRTEEN
COMPONENTS OF BUNDLERABBIT

> ❝ The whole is more than the sum of its parts.

SOME OLD GREEK DUDE NAMED
ARISTOTLE

BUNDLERABBIT IS AN EBOOK BUNDLING PLATFORM. *THIS chapter explains each of BundleRabbit's major components and focuses on the Content Marketplace.*

A PICTURE OF HOW IT WORKS

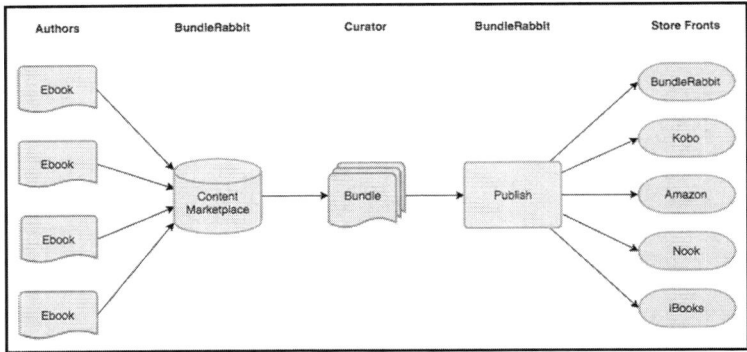

Authors upload their ebooks to BundleRabbit. These ebooks appear in BundleRabbit's Content Marketplace. Curators pull ebooks from the Content Marketplace to build bundles and then use BundleRabbit to publish these bundles on various storefronts.

It really is that simple.

YOUR EBOOK CONTENT IS ALWAYS PRIVATE

When you upload your ebooks to BundleRabbit, you must provide a cover image, set up the metadata, and upload the ebook file. (We'll get into more of the details about this in the next chapter.)

When ebooks are uploaded to BundleRabbit, nobody has access to your actual content.

Curators and authors can see your book's cover in the Content Marketplace. They can read your sales blurb. They can even download a preview if one has been provided, but they don't have access to the actual ebook.

The only time your ebook becomes available is once your ebook is part of a bundle. Then all the participants of the bundle can download their contributor's copy of the box set. And, of course, customers buying the bundle will receive your ebook.

THE CONTENT MARKETPLACE

Both authors and curators have access to the Content Marketplace when they're signed into BundleRabbit. Here they can search through hundreds of ebooks in the marketplace.

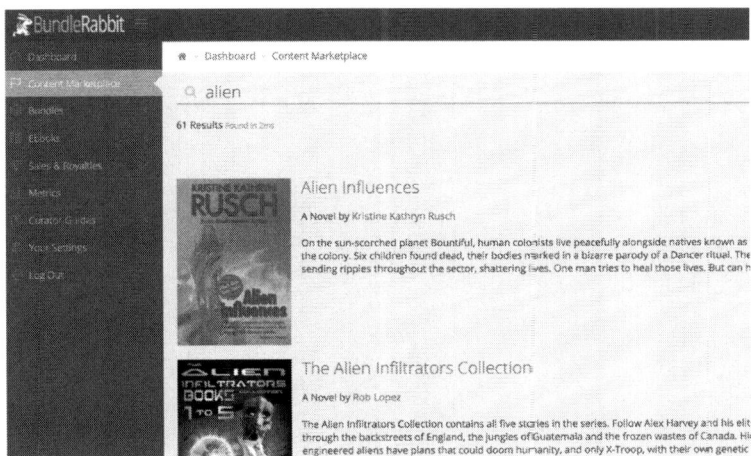

Drilling down on an ebook in the marketplace displays the details about the ebook.

There's a lot of information in the Content Marketplace. You can even see similar ebooks and other works by the author and drill down into those ebooks.

The Content Marketplace design allows curators to explore the available ebooks quickly, thus allowing them to efficiently build their bundles.

❄

YOU DON'T HAVE TO BE IN THE CONTENT MARKETPLACE

Authors can opt out of placing their ebooks in BundleRabbit's Content Marketplace. This makes their ebook invisible to curators and other authors. The only way to be bundled when not in the marketplace is for the curator to contact the author personally and request an ebook.

❋

REQUESTS TO BE BUNDLED

Just because an ebook is uploaded to BundleRabbit doesn't mean the book will automatically be bundled. No. The curator *Sends a Request* and then the author says either *Yes or No.*

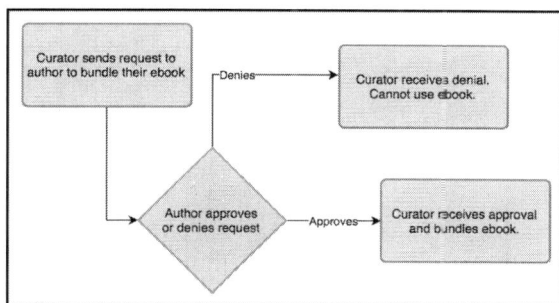

Like everywhere else in BundleRabbit, the author has the final decision what happens with their ebook. The ebook is, after all, the author's intellectual property.

PUBLISHING BUNDLES

When a curator publishes a bundle, the gears start turning and many things happen:

- Specific artwork for the bundle is created. This includes a montage of covers, a cover fan, the 3d box set image, and ads for Facebook and Twitter.
- The box set(s) for the bundle are created.
- The deliverables are set up to flow through BookFunnel.
- The bundle is published on the specified storefronts.

Much of this is automated, but BundleRabbit manually verifies and assembles some items, such as the ads.

One of the final steps in the publishing process is for the curator to review the box set before publishing is finalized.

Generally, it takes two business days for a bundle at BundleRabbit to be ready for the curator's final review. Curators should schedule bundles to be published at least a week in advance.

CHAPTER FOURTEEN
WHAT AUTHORS NEED

> Standing out as a writer today requires more than a bright idea and limpid prose. Authors need to become businesspeople as well.

DAVE MORRIS, AUTHOR OF
GAMEBOOKS, NOVELS, AND COMICS.

THIS CHAPTER EXPLAINS HOW TO GET A BUNDLERABBIT author account and what authors need to provide.

JOINING BUNDLERABBIT

Signing up with BundleRabbit couldn't be easier. Just go to BundleRabbit.com/register, fill out your name, email address, and password (twice), and click the big [JOIN] button.

That's it. You're a member. You should receive a *Welcome to*

BundleRabbit email within moments, but there are no additional links to click or other verifications for your account.

This is the basic membership level. The only thing you can do with a basic membership is view any bundles you've purchased. To be able to upload your ebooks, you must get an author account.

To get an author account:

1. Log on to BundleRabbit
2. Click the How to get an author account link under Other Areas on your dashboard.
3. Hit the [Click Here to Get Started] button.
4. Agree to the Author Agreement.

Easy to do. Once you have an Author account, new areas appear on your dashboard.

- **Sales & Metrics** – Where you can see your sales figures, royalties, and visitor statistics.
- **Content Marketplace** – Where you can browse the hundreds of ebooks other authors have made available for bundling.
- **Your Ebooks** – Where you upload and manage your ebooks.

❄

ALL BUNDLERABBIT MEMBERSHIPS ARE FREE!

BundleRabbit strongly believes in the dictum *Money Flows to the Author*. There are no additional charges or fees to be a member, no matter what membership level you have.

❄

CREATE NEW EBOOK WIZARD

To make the process of uploading your ebook as easy as possible, BundleRabbit provides a *Create New Ebook Wizard*. To start click the CREATE NEW EBOOK link from your dashboard.

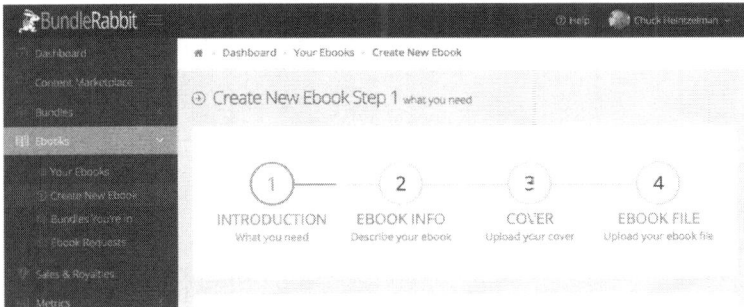

WHAT IS REQUIRED

In order to upload your ebook to BundleRabbit, you need to provide the following:

- General information about the ebook such as title, retail price, and keywords.
- A sales blurb for your ebook.

- A cover image for your ebook (preferably 1667 pixels wide by 2500 pixels high).
- An ebook file, specifically an .EPUB file, a .MOBI file, or a ZIPPED VELLUM file (we'll discuss the zipped Vellum file in a moment). You only need to provide one of these formats.

You'll also be able to specify categories for your ebook, decide whether to show the ebook in the Content Marketplace, and a adjust few other settings.

When in doubt about what a particular setting does, click the [HELP] button at the top of most BundleRabbit pages. The Help page should answer all of your questions.

BUNDLERABBIT-STYLED EPUB

To ensure your ebook file bundles well with others, BundleRabbit reviews every ebook and restyles it as needed. This is a combination manual/automatic process and as such, only a few manuscripts can be processed each day.

Your ebook is placed in a processing queue, where it can remain for days.

Don't worry, though. When your ebook is selected for a bundle, if it's still in the queue, it will be processed immediately, before the bundle is published.

This only applies to .EPUB and .MOBI files. If you provide a ZIPPED VELLUM file, then your ebook skips the queue and does not need to be processed.

ZIPPED VELLUM FILES

At BundleRabbit, it's all about producing high quality box sets so the reader has the best reading experience possible. Because of the variety of formatting and styles individual .EPUB and .MOBI files have, they must be reviewed and restyled.

Not so with Vellum files. A Vellum file easily bundles with others and adopts the style of the bundle as a whole.

To create a ZIPPED VELLUM file, do the following:

- Locate your .VELLUM file in Mac's Finder.
- Right click on the file and choose the COMPRESS FILENAME.VELLUM option.
- This will create a FILENAME.VELLUM.ZIP file that can be uploaded to BundleRabbit.

YOUR EBOOK PREVIEW

After you've uploaded an ebook to BundleRabbit, you can optionally add a preview. This can either be a PDF Preview (recommended) or a Text Preview.

To do this, go to the "Ebook File" section of your ebook in BundleRabbit.

The advantage of providing a preview is that this preview is available to curators, so they can get a feel for your book. It's also available to customers viewing bundles your ebook is part of.

THE EBOOK SPINE IMAGE

Optionally, you can also provide an image of the spine of your ebook. A spine is a fictitious representation of what your book's physical spine would look like. In BundleRabbit, the spine is always figured to be 1.25 inches thick.

1.25 IN. SPINE

BundleRabbit rotates your spine image to create a 3D Box Set image of the bundle containing your book.

Example Spines

❊

IF YOU DO NOT PROVIDE A SPINE IMAGE...

...then BundleRabbit will create one the first time your ebook is bundled. But it is recommended that you do this yourself so you can make your spine look exactly like you want it to look

CHAPTER FIFTEEN
WHAT CURATORS DO

" Organizing and publishing a bundle with multiple authors is a bit like herding cats.

CHUCK HEINTZELMAN

THIS CHAPTER IS ONE BIG LIST OF WHAT CURATORS DO AT BundleRabbit.

CURATORS DEFINE THE BUNDLE'S CONCEPT AND VISION

The curator comes up with the concept for the bundle. Is it a themed bundle? Is there another concept behind the bundle?

They define their vision and communicate this vision to the authors in the bundle. In fact, when authors receive requests from curators to be bundled, the request contains the curator's VISION FOR THE BUNDLE.

CURATORS SELECT AND ORGANIZE THE EBOOKS

In the Content Marketplace, they find ebooks that will potentially fit their bundle. Then they send requests to authors and follow up on those requests.

As the ebooks are approved for the bundle, they put them in the order they'll appear in the bundle.

If the bundle has an entry-level option (a lower-priced bundle containing only a portion of the ebooks from the full bundle), they decide which ebooks will be in this entry-level bundle.

CURATORS PROVIDE IMAGES

Curators select or provide the bundle's background image. The background image appears as the backdrop on sales pages for the bundle at BundleRabbit.

The curator also provides the 2D Cover image for the bundle. This is the cover image used when selling the bundle at Kobo, Amazon, Nook, and iBooks.

The curator may also provide additional images for authors to use to advertise the bundle on the authors' blog, Facebook, Twitter, and so forth.

CURATORS REVIEW THE BOX SET

As the final step before the bundle is published, the curator reviews the box set and verifies the bundle's quality.

CURATORS DETERMINE WHEN AND WHERE THE BUNDLE IS PUBLISHED

Curators set the publication date for the bundle.

They decide where the bundle is published. Is the bundle only for sale at BundleRabbit? Or is it also available at Amazon, Kobo, Nook, and iBooks? If available outside BundleRabbit, when is it available?

When the bundle is finished, the curator unpublishes the bundle.

CURATORS DETERMINE PRICES AND SALES PERIODS

Curators decide what the bundle sells for.

After the bundle is published, curators decide when the bundle goes on sale at discounted prices and how long the sale lasts.

CURATORS FACILITATE COMMUNICATION BETWEEN THE AUTHORS

This is probably the most important curator duty, helping authors communicate. Whether it's through an email list, or using BundleRabbit's sharing features, curators are the ones who start the communication ball rolling.

Curators set the example for the level of communication that occurs within the bundle's mini-community.

CURATORS PROMOTE THE BUNDLE

Curators promote the bundle on their blog, or social media, etc. Curators often come up with other exciting ways to promote the bundle.

CURATORS MANAGE BUNDLE COUPONS

Curators can create coupons to give to authors for promoting the bundle. Promotions such as "Share this post on Facebook before tomorrow to enter a free drawing for this bundle" are facilitated through coupons. (Note: Coupons are only good through BundleRabbit, not through outside channels such as Kobo.)

CURATORS RECEIVE A 5% ROYALTY

For all that curators do, they receive a 5% royalty of sold bundles. (Authors receive 70% distributed evenly across all authors.)

SOME CURATORS DO EVEN MORE

Sometimes curators do even more than listed above. They might coordinate promotions between authors on a shared spreadsheet. Maybe they'll set up pages for the bundle on Facebook or Goodreads. Or they might even guest blog about the bundle.

Point is, curators do a lot. They're the magicians behind the bundle.

> " Be a yardstick of quality. Some people aren't used
> to an environment where excellence is expected.

STEVE JOBS

THIS CHAPTER EXPLAINS SERVICES BUNDLERABBIT PROVIDES.

CONTENT MARKETPLACE

BundleRabbit's Content Marketplace is an open marketplace, where anyone who holds the right to an ebook can be matched with curators interested in bundling their ebook into bundles to sell.

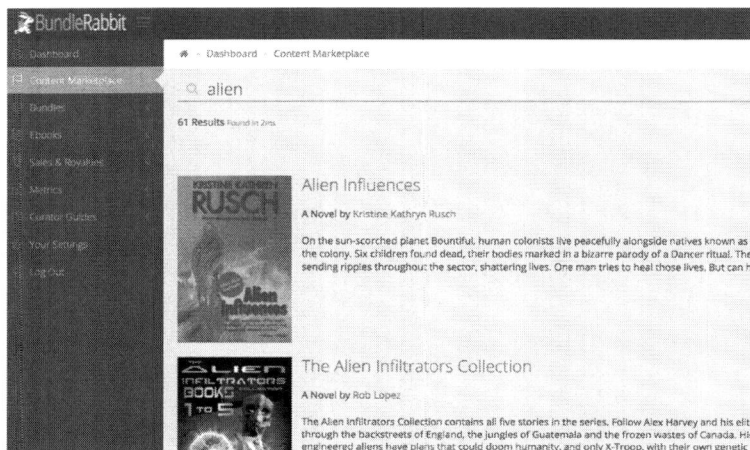

There are hundreds of authors and ebooks in the marketplace.

THE BUNDLING

BundleRabbit makes bundling easy for curators. The complexity of managing, maintaining, publishing, selling, and tracking bundles happens behind the scenes.

ADDITIONAL ARTWORK

BundleRabbit provides additional artwork for every bundle. This artwork is available to the curator and authors in the bundle for marketing and as a base for creating additional artwork.

A Cover Montage is provided, showing the covers from each ebook within the bundle.

A 3D Box Set image is provided.

AND A FAN OF ALL THE COVERS IS PROVIDED.

Additionally, sometimes BundleRabbit will provide ad images for Facebook and Twitter.

PROMPT PAYMENT

BundleRabbit pays royalties owed each month on or before the 5th of the month. For sales occurring on BundleRabbit, this occurs quickly. For example, if a bundle sells on July 29th, authors receive their share of that sale no later than August 5th.

For outside sales, there's a two-month delay in payment. This is because BundleRabbit doesn't pay authors until it receives payment. Thus if a bundle sells on Amazon on July 29th, Amazon doesn't pay BundleRabbit until around September 30th, so authors will be paid for this by October 5th.

BundleRabbit pays all royalties through PayPal and only when the balance owed is $10 or more.

METRICS

BundleRabbit provides a number of charts displaying various metrics so authors and curators can track bundles and ebooks in various ways.

You can see the sales counts for bundles over time, or the number of visitors to a bundle's sales page over time.

For ebooks, you can see the number of times an ebook was viewed in the Content Marketplace for any given day. You can even see the number of visitors to your ebook's *Public Page* (explained in detail in Chapter 19).

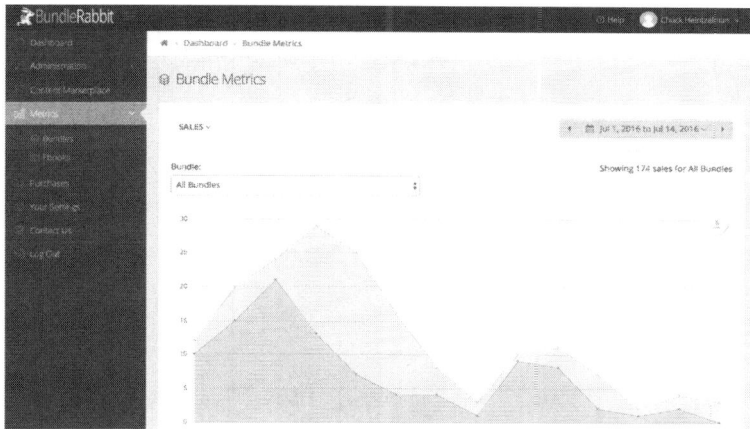

BUNDLERABBIT STOREFRONT

BundleRabbit also provides a slick storefront for users to discover and purchase bundles. Curators can set up a price slider for their bundle, allowing customers to pay what they want. If the bundle has associated charities, then customers can designate 10% of their purchase to go to a charity.

CHAPTER SEVENTEEN
TIPS FOR GETTING INTO A BUNDLE

> The advice I would give to someone is to not take anyone's advice.

EDDIE MURPHY

ONE OF THE MOST COMMON QUESTION I RECEIVE FROM authors at BundleRabbit is "How do I get into a bundle?" This chapter provides the best advice I can give on that question.

FULL AND ACCURATE METADATA

Metadata is all the information authors provide to describe an ebook. This includes the title, keywords, categories, and so forth.

The ebook's metadata determines how the ebook is found when it is searched for in the Content Marketplace. Since the main way curators discover books is through searching the Content

Marketplace, it's imperative the metadata is not only completely filled in, but that it's accurate as well.

BundleRabbit algorithms use this metadata to determine how similar ebooks are to each other. Thus when a curator explores someone else's ebook in the Content Marketplace, the chances of them noticing your book in the *Similar Ebooks* section fully depends on the metadata.

Think of it this way...

Good Metadata = Better Chance for Curator Discovery

THE EBOOK COVER

The second most important item for getting into a bundle is the ebook's cover.

Ebook cover design is a vast topic and cannot be covered in depth here. Here are a few tips about ebooks covers:

- Make sure the cover is compelling at thumbnail size. This is how curators first see the cover.
- Fonts such as Comic Sans or Papyrus immediately flag the cover as amateurish.
- Garish colors or gradients also come off amateurish.
- Limit the number of different fonts on the cover to two.
- Less is more. Minimalism is a timeless style.
- The cover should fit the genre. This includes the type of art work, mood, and font.

- Just like with a physical book, the cover's job is to get the book picked up (or in this case clicked on).
- When in doubt, hire it out. Don't do your own cover unless you know you'll do a good job.

THE SALES BLURB

A curator looks at an ebook's sales blurb through two different lenses:

1. Does it sell them on the book?
2. Will it help sell potential bundle customers on the book?

Here are a few tips for the sales blurb:

- Only use the active voice.
- Keep the blurb short. Aim to 4 to 8 sentences across 3 to 4 paragraphs.
- Do not use boring plot summaries.

❄

A HIDDEN SALES BLURB GIFT

In BundleRabbit's members area, go into your ebooks, pick one of your ebooks, and click to the SALES INFO. When you hit the [HELP] button at the top of this page, you'll discover a gift that helps writing sales blurb.

❄

PROVIDE A PREVIEW

Once a curator discovers your ebook (through the ebook's metadata), clicks on the cover, and finds the sales blurb intriguing, often they'll see if you have a preview. If you have a preview and the curator likes it, they're more likely to send you a request to be bundled.

BundleRabbit makes it easy to upload a preview for your ebook.

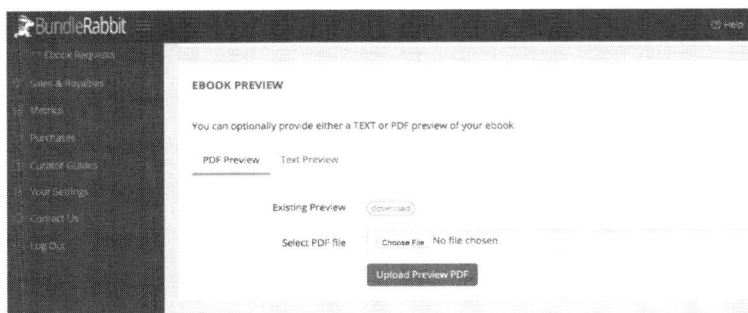

Just go to your ebook in BundleRabbit, click on EBOOK FILE, and scroll down to upload either a PDF Preview or Text Preview.

WHO YOU KNOW

Let's face it, one of the most common ways to be included in a bundle is when the curator already knows you. They know your work, the quality and style, and how it fits into the bundle their building.

They also know how you promote. They know your social presence. They know if you have a newsletter.

Promotion is in the back of every curator's mind. The success of the bundle largely depends on how well the authors promote the bundle.

CREATE YOUR OWN BUNDLE

The only 100% absolute way to guarantee you'll be in a bundle is to curate it yourself.

BundleRabbit makes bundle curation easy.

And, as mentioned in *Chapter 11 – Bundling as a Mini-Community,* there's an aspect of networking involved when you curate or participate in a bundle. I like to think of this as "Networking for Introverts."

And think of this: once you've curated a bundle, then everyone participating in the bundle knows you. They know how you work. Which takes you back to the previous section of this chapter, *Who You Know.*

> Sharing is good, and with digital technology, sharing is easy.

RICHARD STALLMAN, SOFTWARE
FREEDOM ACTIVIST

THIS CHAPTER EXPLAINS THE TOOLS BUNDLERABBIT PROVIDES to facilitate sharing within the bundle mini-communities.

MESSAGE BOARD

Each bundle has its own message board. Curators can access the message board for their bundle by going to the bundle's overview and clicking on MESSAGES. Authors access the message board by clicking the BUNDLES YOU'RE IN link from their Dashboard and then clicking on the [MESSAGES] button for the bundle.

Once you're into the Message Board, you'll see a list of available topics.

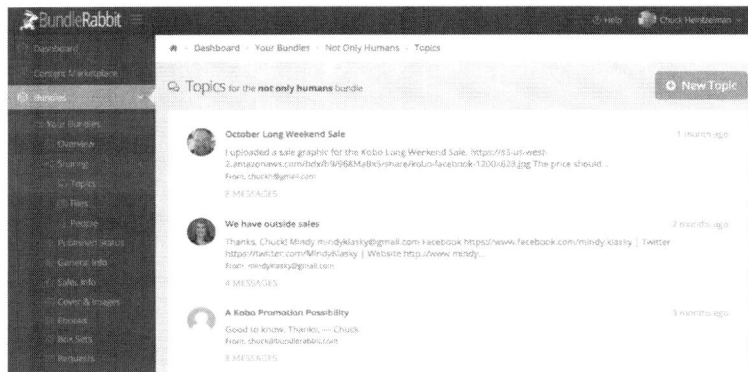

From this screen, click on any of the topics to view the messages within the topic. Or click the [New Topic] button to create a message with a new topic.

When you're viewing the messages for a topic, the oldest message appears at the top. Scroll to the bottom of the page to view the latest messages.

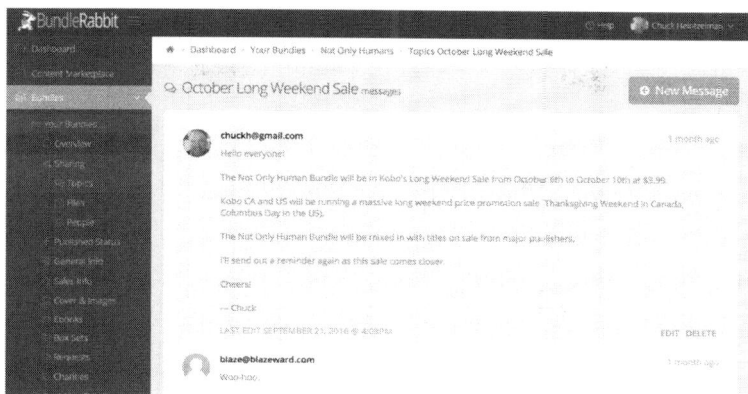

To add a new message within the topic, click the [NEW MESSAGE] button.

EMAIL NOTICES

Whenever somebody creates a new message within a bundle you're participating in, you'll receive an email containing the message.

BundleRabbit Messages
[Not Only Humans] Just a little test
To: Chuck Heintzelman

Inbox - chuckh@gmail.com   7:45 PM

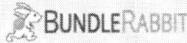

BUNDLERABBIT

Hi Someone,

This is just a test. I want to **Make Sure** that a few things work with the email. That a long line will wrap okay, etc.

That is all,
Chuck

Posted by: Chuck Heintzelman

View All Messages

You are receiving this email because a new message has been posted to a bundle you're participating in. Turn off email notifications by disabling **Share Notifications** in the **Notifications** tab of **Your Settings** screen.

Replying to this email will add a new message to this topic.

Replying to this email will add a new message to the topic. You don't even have to log in to BundleRabbit to participate in the bundle's mini-community.

If you don't want to receive emails each time a new message is added, you can change this in YOUR SETTINGS at BundleRab-bit. Click the NOTIFICATIONS tab.

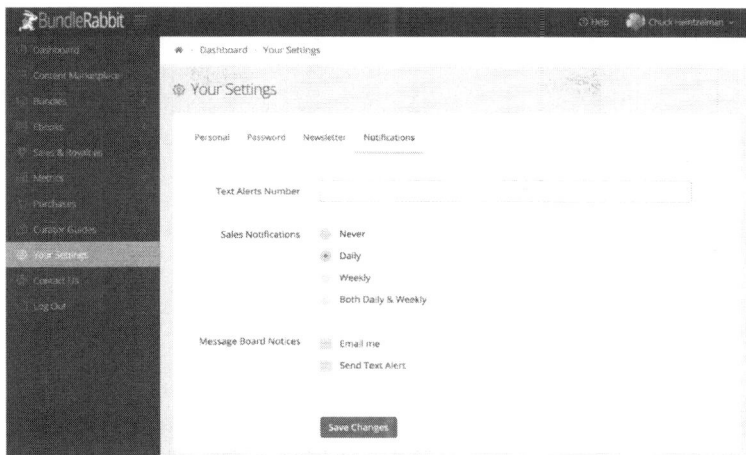

Here you can also change your settings to receive a text alert when new messages occur.

SHARED FILES

BundleRabbit also provides a common area for sharing files associated with bundles.

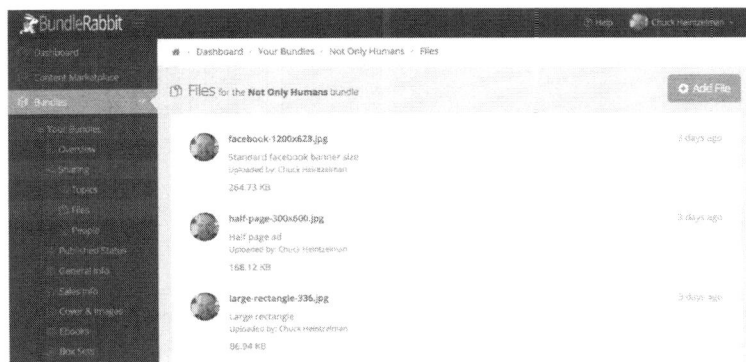

This is a great place to share artwork, ads created for the bundle, sales copy, and other related information.

PEOPLE

Besides the messages and files that are shared between bundle participants, there's also another handy area, the PEOPLE section. A table of everyone participating in the bundle is displayed here.

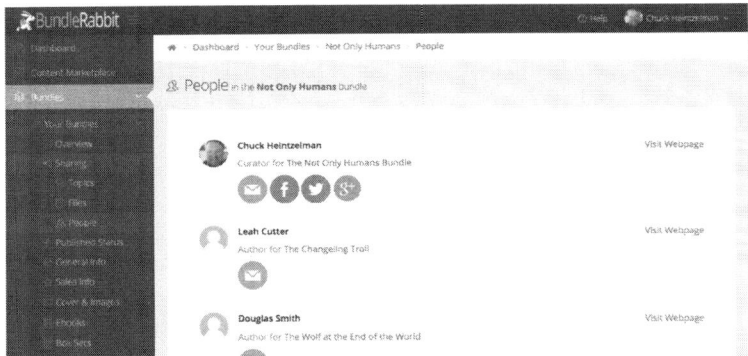

From this screen you can view each person's role in the bundle, their email and website, and any social media they've set up.

Make sure you friend everyone on Facebook, follow everyone who has Twitter, and add those with Google+ to your circles.

> " There are no traffic jams on the extra mile.

ZIG ZIGLAR, AUTHOR, SALESMAN,
MOTIVATIONAL SPEAKER

THIS CHAPTER COVERS DIFFERENT WAYS BUNDLERABBIT ADDS *to an author's discoverability.*

THE BUNDLE ITSELF

When a bundle you're in is purchased, readers see your story. But if you do it correctly they'll also have multiple paths (bread-crumbs) back to you.

Your ebook within the bundle should contain:

- An ABOUT THE AUTHOR page with a link to your website.

- An ALSO BY page with links to each story.
- A link to sign up for your newsletter.
- A Preview of the next book in the series or other novel by you. With, of course, a link to buy it at the end.
- Links to all of your social media.

Links, links, links. Do you see the pattern here?

❄

LINKS TO STOREFRONTS IN YOUR EBOOK

When your ebook has a link to a specific storefront such as Kobo, this link only appears when the BundleRabbit box set is sold at that storefront. Vendors don't allow links to their competition.
If the link goes to your own site, that's fine. The link is retained across each different storefront.
Or, if you provide a ZIPPED VELLUM file to BundleRabbit, then each storefront can have its own link within its version of the box set. Another reason you should provide ZIPPED VELLUM files to BundleRabbit when possible.

❄

BUNDLERABBIT'S BUNDLE SALES PAGE

When you're in a bundle, the sales page at BundleRabbit shows information about the bundle with the covers from each book in the bundle.

When an interested reader sees your cover and clicks on it, they'll see additional information about you and your ebook. A link back to your website is provided here. Customers have one more way to find your site.

This sales page has information about both you and your book, providing search engines another way to find this bundle and thus find you.

Since authors in the bundle are linking to this page from their blogs, social media, and through other marketing techniques, there are many more second- and third-level links for readers to discover you.

EBOOK VENDOR SALES PAGES

When you're in a bundle sold at Kobo, Amazon, Nook, and iBooks, their storefronts provide additional ways to find you.

Readers find the bundle on these storefronts through searching, browsing, READER ALSO BOUGHT links, and other promotions on the storefront.

BundleRabbit always includes the bundle's table of contents, with your title and name, in the box set's description, to aid with searches on the vendor's site.

The bundle also becomes one more title in the list of titles associated with your author name.

❄

CLAIMING THE BUNDLE IN AMAZON

AMAZON ALLOWS ONLY TEN AUTHOR NAMES TO BE associated with an ebook on their store. If your book isn't associated, you can still claim it with a tiny bit of effort.

1. Log in to Author Central at Amazon. (If you haven't set up Author Central, you'll need to do that first.)
2. If you don't see the bundle in your list of books, then hit the [ADD MORE BOOKS] button.
3. Search for the bundle, and when found, click the [THIS IS MY BOOK] button.
4. A window will pop up presenting the list of authors in the book. If you see your name, then click the [THIS IS ME] button; otherwise click the CONTACT US link and fill out the form.

It usually only takes a day for Amazon to link you to the bundle.

❆

DAILY EBOOK SPOTLIGHT

Most days, BundleRabbit emails subscribers who want to see more information about the deals at BundleRabbit. This email highlights an ebook or two in active bundles. Links are provided to the bundle everywhere it's sold.

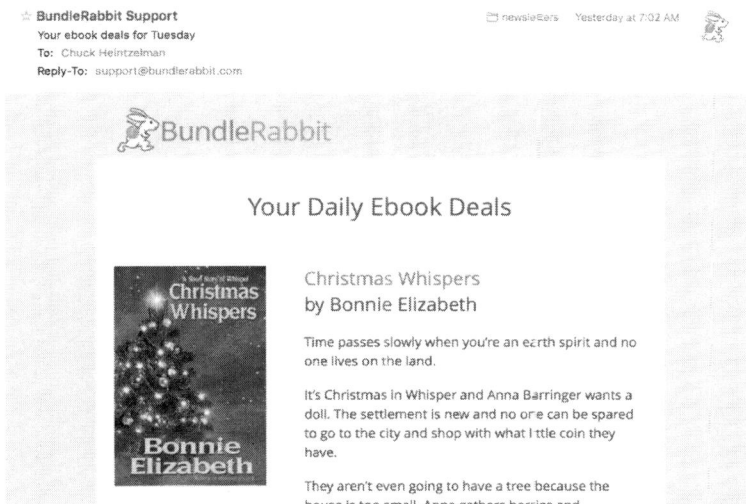

The last ten days of Daily Ebook Spotlights are also displayed at BundleRabbit's website.

PUBLIC EBOOK PAGES

Here's a cool discoverability feature BundleRabbit provides that doesn't even require your ebook to be bundled.

On BundleRabbit's SALES INFO page for your ebook, there's an EBOOK PAGE IS PUBLIC setting. Enabling this puts another web page out on the interwebs with links not only to your website, but to social media you've associated with the book.

This Public Ebook Page is optimized and submitted to the search engines. People browsing the BundleRabbit pages have access to hundreds of these Public Ebook Pages.

> We're all in this together—when one writer succeeds, all writers succeed.
>
> LISA GARDNER, #1 NEW YORK TIMES
> BESTSELLING AUTHOR

Make sure you fill out at the social links for your book to get the most benefit from Public Ebook Pages.

This is just one way BundleRabbit goes the extra mile.

WHERE TO GO NEXT

66 Action is the foundational key to all success.

PABLO PICASSO

HOPEFULLY NOW YOU UNDERSTAND WHAT EBOOK bundling is, how to do it, and the benefits ebook bundling provides to today's authors. Ebook bundling is not a panacea, but simply another tool in today's author's arsenal of promotion and publishing tools.

But it is a tool that every author should use.

So what are the next steps?

Here are two simple action items I urge you to perform.

STEP 1 – REVIEW YOUR INVENTORY FOR BUNDLING OPPORTUNITIES

Look at all the books you've written. Can you create some collections? Short story collections? First in Series collections? Review *Chapter 3 – Example Bundles* for ideas.

Build every single-author bundles you can. Get them selling everywhere ebooks are sold.

Expand your inventory!

STEP 2 – UPLOAD YOUR TITLES TO BUNDLERABBIT

Create an action plan to upload your titles to BundleRabbit. Get them there so you can take advantage of multi-author bundles.

BundleRabbit is the easiest way that exists to do this.

You might even want to curate a bundle or two.

❄

THE WIBBOW TEST

AS A PARTING THOUGHT IN THIS BOOK, I'M SHARING A WORD coined by Scott William Carter: WIBBOW. It's an acronym standing for Would I Be Better Off Writing?

This is the question to ask yourself when doing some activity that's not writing. Use WIBBOW as the litmus test when doing anything for your writing business.

As I mentioned back in *Chapter 9 – Pricing and Selling Bundles*, I don't set all the individual prices for the 50+ stores at iBooks. For me, this doesn't pass the WIBBOW test.

Creating bundles to expand your reach is important, but you should not focus on bundling to the complete exclusion of writing. Schedule time away from your writing to take care of your bundling projects and other administration tasks.

You should never stop writing, never stop producing of new work.

And then bundling it.

ALSO BY CHUCK HEINTZELMAN

SHORT STORIES

Freshly Ghost

The Jaws of the Manō

The Train Bandits

Tailfeathers Up, Beak Down

Pact of the Banshee

Wizard Lottery

City Shadows

And Through the Haze You See Your God

Mad Goldilocks

Three Strikes

The Babysitter

The Djin's Box

It Don't Taste Like Slug

The Luckiest Man in the Universes

Memory Fades

Trunk of Caramel

Three Wishes and a Bath

Cleopatra's Medallion

The Death Gerbil

The Messiah Machine

COLLECTIONS

Stuttering in the Dark

Expelled Figments

NON FICTION

Getting Stuff Done with Laravel 4

Laravel 5.1 Beauty

The Author's Guide to Ebook Bundling

Chuck Heintzelman spends his days architecting software systems for businesses ranging from Fortune 500 companies to Mom and Pop stores. He believes in simple and elegant software which hides internal complexities from the user.

When he's not writing code, Chuck writes quirky short stories, usually with some sort of fantastical element. He's as surprised by this as anyone. Even after dozens of stories published he still stays up too late at night, feverishly working on the next tale.

He lives in the Pacific Northwest with his beautiful wife and their daughters.

BundleRabbit is the premier DIY ebook bundling service. BundleRabbit helps readers save money on ebooks by providing authors with the tools to bundle their books together and offer them at a discount.

Visit BundleRabbit.com to see the latest bundles.

Sign up for the BundleRabbit Newsletter and be notified of great ebook deals!

THE WITCHES'S BREW BUNDLE

Magic sparks and cauldrons bubble;

Potions bring love, and curses bring trouble.

What if magic could help track down a murderer?

Can a young, untrained witch save her people from a dark wizard –
and at what cost to herself?

Does a young woman's dreams really predict the future? If so, is there
any way to change what she foresees?

And what might an independent young witch look for when house
hunting?

Witches. Warlocks. Wizards. Familiars...

Enter twenty different worlds of magic and enchantment.

THE OUT OF THIS WORLD BUNDLE

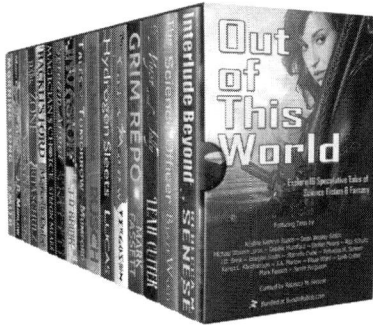

Explore the future and the universe with this exciting bundle of science fiction & fantasy short stories, novellas, and novels. Discover how people will survive, and thrive, as they encounter challenges in outer space or deal with struggles here on Earth.

Mystery and adventure, drama and fear, technology and magic, all have their place in these exciting speculative stories.

Blast away with these 16 fantastical tales to parts unknown and out of this world!

THE FANTASY IN THE CITY BUNDLE

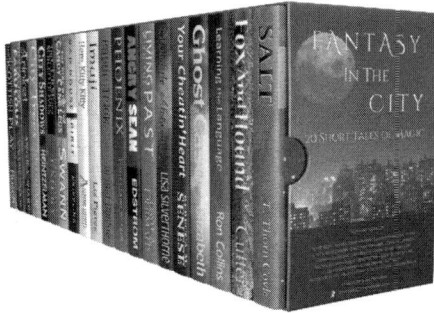

What if magic were right in front of you every day, but hidden from your sight?

For all you know, it is.

Maybe the reason you love the tasty creations from the nearby chocolate shop is that one of the ingredients is magic.

Perhaps some of the dreadlocks of the beautiful young girl you saw at the grocery store are snakes, not hair.

The woman you just passed on the street appeared to be on her cell phone, but she might really be speaking with a ghost.

How do you know for sure?

Witches. Ghosts. Faeries. Monsters. Magic...

Enter twenty different worlds, each with a different flavor of magic.

This bundle contains 20 urban fantasy stories about hidden magic in everyday life.

DISCOVER THESE AND MANY MORE BUNDLES AT
BUNDLERABBIT.COM

Printed in Great Britain
by Amazon